Stockholmed

11 years surviving domestic violence

Stockholm syndrome

–noun Psychiatry.

Definition

Stockholm syndrome refers to a group of psychological symptoms that occur in some persons in a captive or hostage situation. It has received considerable media publicity in recent years because it has been used to explain the behavior of such well-known kidnapping victims as Patty Hearst (1974) and Elizabeth Smart (2002). The term takes its name from a bank robbery in Stockholm, Sweden, in August 1973. The robber took four employees of the bank (three women and one man) into the vault with him and kept them hostage for 131 hours. After the employees were finally released, they appeared to have formed a paradoxical emotional bond with their captor; they told reporters that they saw the police as their enemy rather than the bank robber, and that they had positive feelings toward the criminal. The syndrome was first named by Nils Bejerot (1921–1988), a medical professor who specialized in addiction research and served as a psychiatric consultant to the Swedish police during the standoff at the bank. Stockholm syndrome is also known as . . . ***Survival Identification Syndrome***.

PROLOGUE:

They say that the third time is a charm. That may be correct; I certainly know that my third marriage is more than a charm. It was, and still is the best thing that ever happened to me. But I'm well past the third time I've started writing this same book. In fact, at this sitting, I'm on number six.

The jerky, on again off again approach to my "Great American Novel" has nothing to do with writer's block, I've never had a problem with that. An idea for a story will bounce around in my brain like Ricochet Rabbit eating speed like candy until it spills out through my fingers and onto my computer. Then, generally, it flows through me like electricity until the slayer of my sleep is seen to fruition. However, I find that this particular gem of literary wisdom will, from time to time, come to a horrible, screaming, irrevocable halt because of the dark shadows of my past that slide up behind me slipping boney ice cold fingers around my brain as I write, and drag my soul back to a chain of events in my life that had eventually added the taste of a gun barrel to my palatable memories.

I've allowed myself to believe, five different times apparently, that the old adage of time being the great healer of all wounds was vaguely accurate. Five different times I've been wrong, because five different times now I've found myself catatonic, fingers trembling as they hovered over my expectant keyboard, reliving one of countless incidents that ended in embarrassment, broken bones, or missing teeth at the hands of a "loving" spouse.

I should explain that sporadically throughout this work the reader will notice the text suddenly changes to italics and is separated from the rest of the work by this ***. This book is written so others whom have either traveled this road, or are currently on it will find some kind of solace in the fact that they are not alone. Additionally, it is important to me that these same people understand that writing this was far from cathartic. The fact is it came close to costing me my life on more than one occasion. These special sections speak to my personal frame of mind as I wrote this manuscript, the fact that I now fight with thoughts of suicide every day, and hopefully let these weary travelers understand that they are not alone in this respect as well. PTSD ain't for pussies.

I've tried to explain this eleven year black hole in my life to family and friends, and almost to a person, (the only two notable exceptions are my current wife and my ex sister-in-law, both survivors of abusive relationships) the reaction I get is "why the hell did you let her do that to you?" Apparently, domestic violence is what happens when a man beats up a woman. If the roles are reversed, the male isn't a victim, he's a pussy.

I've listened to people's opinion about why anyone stays in a relationship like this and so far, from expert to novice they are all wrong. I personally have been told that on some level I must have been "grooving" on the violence or I would have left. I've heard victims of abuse say the reason they stay in a relationship is because they love the abuser too much to leave, and I can say without hesitation that *love* has nothing to do with it. "Love" is the term abuse victims use when they have no idea why they're doing what they're doing. "Love" is what the abuser beats these people over the head with on a daily basis. "Love," used in the context of a conversation with an abused person, should read, "You'll never understand anyway; you can't help me so just leave me alone until you can." Hearing the term "love" might make a person walk away from an abused person shaking their head in disbelief, but at least it makes them walk away.

All of that being said, I will try once more to tell my story, twenty years after I ran away from my nightmare, in the hopes that it might make some type of social change.

I sincerely doubt that it will.

One

The enormity of dreadful emotion flowed over me as if a truckload of sand and molasses had been dumped on my head. I wasn't supposed to be here. Not anymore, all of this was supposed to be behind me. I knew in my mind that I needed to be someplace else . . . someplace specific . . . someplace other than here . . . someplace that was much nicer than this.

I craved it, every fiber of my physical and emotional being clawed for it. I knew that if I didn't get to that place, wherever it might be, immediately, I would suffocate in the blackness of the depressing emotional pit I was standing in.

Then, she was there, standing in front of me with that downtrodden look of the perpetual victim. All I wanted to do was punch her right in her emotionless face. I needed to do that just as badly as I needed to be someplace else, but I couldn't. She was moaning on and on about some wrong; real or perceived, that I had committed against her. I was trying to explain myself, thinking that in some convoluted way I would be able to assuage her hurt feelings. At the same time I knew unquestionably that the closer I got to a rational breakthrough, the closer she came to reaching deep into her perpetual "victim demeanor" in order to instantly turn into something far more violent and destructive.

Some place deep in my subconscious I knew that this lunatic was no longer my wife, just as I knew that my real wife was actually someplace else waiting for me. My mind screamed to just walk out, put this all behind me and go back to the person that I loved more than life itself. The person that I knew was some place waiting for me, just as I knew that she would be completely destroyed if she knew where I was. No matter if I wanted to be there or not.

There was an incessant knocking at the door.

What door?

Was there a door somewhere in this . . . whatever the hell it was I was in?

In front of me, this woman just kept droning on and on, touching every last nerve in my body, and making my skin feel like it had been sandpapered. My every weakness and every indiscretion was laid bare leaving me emotionally naked and exposed.

That knocking . . . .

That droning that was becoming increasingly more threatening . . . .

"Just shut the hell up!" I finally screamed.

The droning stopped and the woman had the look of a serial killer who hadn't satisfied her bloodlust in quite some time.

She moved toward me.

"Come on, do it, come on," I said again. My fists were clenched tight at my side. "Come on, Hit me! I dare you, hit me!"

She stopped . . . and pulled the shotgun out of nowhere.

"Do it," I said darkly. "Just finally do it, or answer that damned door."

She smiled…and pulled the trigger.

My eyes snapped open and I was consumed by total darkness. My heart was pounding in my chest in a rhythm that nearly matched the knocking on the door.

Door?

Apparently I was in a room.

Slowly, I began to realize what reality I was in now. The squat, round room I was in was coming into focus in nondescript gray and black shadows. I could make out rough latticework running all the way around the outside wall, and there was a hole in the roof with a pipe sticking out of it.

The knock again.

"Yes?" I said in the dark.

I could hear a woman's voice responding to me, but I had no earthly idea what language she was speaking.

"What?' I said again.

"Fire?" the thickly accented voice called back through the door.

Fire?

What the hell?

Oh, yeah, that's right. Fire.

"Yes, yes, please come in," I said.

A very small door opened, letting in a little dusky light. The opening couldn't have been more than four feet high and about 2 ½ feet wide. It was actually more of a square hobbit hole than it was a door. A small, Asian-looking woman came in, barely needing to bend over. She was carrying an arm load of wood and an infectious smile that radiated even in this dim light.

"Fire for you," she said again.

"Yes, please, that would be very nice."

Across the room, a body stirred beneath a thick quilt in a

11

wooden framed bed that had been painted bright orange and adorned with hand painted flowers. I smiled absently in the darkness. Yes, as odd as it may seem to normal people, this was where I was supposed to be. I was in a yurt camp in Northern Mongolia, and the lump resting comfortably under the covers across the room was my best friend and wife of fifteen years.

The Mongolian woman made herself busy stoking up a fire in the timeless old stove that sat in the middle of the round room on the wooden floor. Fire marshals in the states would have had a kitten if they ever saw this heating device, or the skinny wire that ran around the room and ended unceremoniously taped to a bare bulb hanging from one of the skinny spoke beams that held the flannel roof up. In the states these things were important, but in Mongolia, no one seemed to care.

I sat on the side of the bed and rubbed my eyes hard to try and squeeze the unchecked hatred out of my mind from the dream a few minutes before. Through the flue hole in the center of the roof, I could see that the beautiful Mongolian sky was beginning to lighten to muted shades of grey and pink. Soon the sun would be rising over Lake Hovsgol and I didn't want to miss it.

Although the direct line from my own brightly painted bed to the charmingly small door was only about six feet, Yurt protocol is very specific about the way one moves thru the room to show respect. As you enter the door, you move to the left and when you leave you continue in that direction until you reach the door. So as I went the long way around, I passed by the small brightly painted tea table that held the beautiful and delicate porcelain tea cups, hot water thermos, and assorted tea bags. Then past the handmade and like-painted chest of drawers, I passed between my sleeping wife and the Mongolian fire lady, and ducked out the tiny entrance to find myself engulfed in the wild beauty of the Siberian Frontier.

A handful of yurts identical to mine lay scattered among the giant majestic Mongolian pine trees. In the dim light, I could see smoke wafting out of most of the flues flinging sparks into the cold morning air. I chuckled to myself; it was amazing to me that the entire country didn't burn down.

A soft, grassy slope rolled away from the clutch of yurts, continued past the meeting hall where we had dinner the night before, and spilled over a line of pebbles that had been worn smooth by the relentless water of the breathtakingly clear lake over the course of countless years. It was not difficult at all to imagine that this was exactly the same scene that the great Mongolian Khans themselves had witnessed hundreds, even thousands of years before. It is not hard to understand how the lake got the name "Dark Blue Pearl of Mongolia."

Behind me, the snow-capped peaks of the Khoridol Saridag Mountains were just beginning to reflect the light of day that had yet to reach the calm, serine shores of the lake. I sat down on an ancient pine stump right at the water's edge, closed my eyes, and sucked the freshness of an untouched wilderness deep into my lungs. One of the Mongolian horse wranglers stood near me soaking in the scene in the same way I was. His hands were stuffed deeply into the pockets of his long riding coat. A beautiful and ornate yellow band of silk served as a belt. Smoke from the ever-present Mongol cigarette built up under the brim of his cowboy hat and softly rolled up the sides, making it look as though his head was on fire.

"сайн уу" I said to him.

He nodded briefly and redirected his stoic gaze out to the most beautiful sunrise that had ever existed on the face of the planet.

I thought I had said "hello," but for all I knew, I might have said "please be sure and butter my Armadillo."

The feelings of the nightmare from just a very few moments before forced their way back into my mind, and I was amazed at just how far I had come since the dark days living in the very real hell that my life had been.

All I wanted to know now was how much longer those horrible dreams were going to invade my life.

TWO

Twenty-Six Years earlier.

I had moved into an apartment close to work and was busy going about the menial tasks of living my life when I met Mary. She was a few years older, attractive, outgoing, and married with three kids. In my twenty-six-year-old, underdeveloped mind the "married" part obviously stamped a giant "THE END" on the chapter of my life that included Mary. I never even began to consider that she might possess other ideas, or an endless stockpile of determination, and the giant sense of self it took to screw over anyone who got in her way until she got what she wanted.

Over the course of several months, I became friends with Mary, her husband, and her kids. They lived in the apartment right below me, and during my free time, we all would participate in softball games, picnics, pool parties, and whatever other community activities might pop up in an environment like this. Mary was always flirty with me, but I never gave it much thought since she was flirty with everybody.

Then, late one night there was a knock on my door, and I was shocked to find Mary standing there.

"There's some things I need to talk to you about," she said.

I couldn't for the life of me think of one single thing that would be so important between a married woman and me that would necessitate a late night conversation.

"Where's your husband?" I said as I let her in.

"He's downstairs watching the kids."

"And does he know that you're up here?"

"Yeah, I told him I wanted to yell at you about something."

"And why are you really here?" I asked as I leaned up against the dining room table.

"I want to get something straight between us."

"What would that be?"

For the next twenty or thirty minutes she paced around the table, gesturing with a punctuating index finger, telling me that she wanted to "be" with me and that there was nothing I could do to stop her. She told me that the only thing left to do was for me to decide when that was going to happen. I had little or nothing to say, and as I look back on that scene, I guess she expected me to sweep her up in my arms and ravish her right there. She kept telling me that her husband was suspicious and that he was probably looking through my peep hole right then trying to see what was going on.

"Well hell yes," I thought. *"I'd be suspicious also."*

When she left, I remember thinking she was going to have to wait for one hell of a long time before I was EVER going to get involved in that mess. I didn't mind being with a woman that had kids, but when I was in the service the guy that was screwing another sailors' wife while the husband was at sea was known as a Jody . . . and I was no Jody. Besides, aside from his drinking and being a general Bozo, I kind of liked her husband.

Apparently my penis was making other plans that I was not privy to.

Life around Mary after that incident was . . . odd. We both made like it had never happened and nothing was said. Then, what seemed at first to be an innocuous event changed my life forever. As I look back on that day, I'm surprised I didn't hear a giant exclamation of a heavenly host ushering in a new age. Mary asked me, in passing as I was on my way to the laundry room, if I would like to go to a local country bar that night with her, her husband and several other people from the complex.

"Sure," I said. What could possibly go wrong there?

THREE

Just like the gold rush of the 19th century, John Travolta and the movie *Urban Cowboy* heralded in a queen's boatload of country-western bars filled with faux cowboys wearing very expensive cowboy hats, even more expensive boots (that would never come close to seeing barn dirt let alone an errant road apple), cheap beer, and bad attitudes. On the arms of these backyard goat ropers were women in painted on jeans, huge fake hair, and huger faux boobs that struggled to free themselves from cute little scrapes of gingham and lace that, on a Barbie doll, could have been called blouses.

The centerpiece of this experiment in social conformity was an electric maiming device dressed up to look like a rodeo bull. Young men loaded down with beer and testosterone could mount this thing in hopes of, A: impressing young women; B: being thrown into a wall or bystander with a bone-jarring stop just before being whisked away to an emergency room; C: Spewing the contents of their stomachs around the room.

This was the backdrop for our innocent outing. Mary's husband and I leaned up against a railing in the back of the bar watching the not-really-country–western show go by. We were beating small talk to death as he hooked himself up to his hops-driven life support system, and I nursed my beer. Mary was the only woman in our group of five or six and she spent her time being passed around on the dance floor between the other men in the group like a 1930's taxi dancer.

At the time, her husband seemed to be oblivious to this.

Then suddenly, "Son-of-a-bitch!" he slurred.

I was shocked out of my disinterest in his conversation, "What?" I asked innocently.

"He just put his fucking hand on her fucking ass!" he said pointing at one of the men in our group that was once again escorting his wife out to the dance floor with his hand planted firmly on her ass.

"Oh," I said. "*Oh shit*" I thought. The ass groping had been going on ever since we got there, but I thought he either hadn't seen it, or hadn't cared. I was wondering how much help I could expect from bystanders when I had to pull these two drunken clowns apart as the fighting started.

Boy was I in the wrong ballpark!

When Mary got back to the group with her ass-groping dance

partner the first words out of her spouse's mouth were exactly what I expected.

"*What the fuck!?*" he yelled indignantly.

The surprising part was that this beer soaked curse/open-ended question was directed right into Mary's face. The groper was totally ignored!

Stoically, Mary stood there waiting for the diatribe to be over. It was painfully obvious that she had been here one too many times before. Even more painful was the fact that all of the rest of us just stood there inspecting our boots as the screaming drunken assault went on.

Right up until he slapped her in the mouth hard enough to knock her back into the groper and stalked off out of the bar to sit on his car...completely unmolested by any of the gentlemen/cowboys in our group. . . .

Or any gentle bystanders that had witnessed the act of violence. . . .

Still, we all stood there not doing a damned thing. Too bad we didn't have the electric bull handy so we could prove our manhood.

I drove away from the bar feeling like a waste of life, and telling myself that if that ever happened again I would handle everything totally different, by God! Little did I know just how soon I would have the chance to prove myself.

I pulled into the driveway of my apartment complex still thinking about what I should have done at the bar. Lost in self-absorbed thoughts of masculine retribution, I paid no attention to the car that had pulled into the driveway in front of me—at least I didn't notice it until the brake lights suddenly came on ,forcing the front of the car to dive to the ground in a gesture of obedience. Irritated, I waited for the driver to get the hell out of my way. This night had already been a giant pain in my ass.

Then several things happened all at once; someone got out of the right side of the car and jumped, spread eagle, onto the hood; I recognized this person as Mary's drunken husband; I recognized the driver as Mary; the drunk rolled off the hood, belted the driver in the mouth through the open window as she pleaded with him to get back in the car. I immediately added the incident to my embarrassing list of "things I'll do different the next time" by slowly backing out of the driveway so I could drive around town until the domestic violence incident posing as an obstruction was conveniently cleared out of my way, and I could reach the comfortable confines of my apartment.

Once again, I was completely free of the musty smell of involvement in "other people's" problems.

At least, I thought it would be comfortable in my apartment. Maybe, at least, I could be confined from the harsh realities of unpredictable public life.

Sometime in what is whimsically known as the wee hours of the morning, as I sat in the dark vowing a change in my personal action the NEXT time . . . by God, I heard a scream in the hallway below my door. I knew who it was: Mary and the drunk were still going at it, and the fight had spilled out into the night, giving all the participants of the "scene" at the bar a third and final chance to redeem ourselves. Six sets of ears listened behind six doors, clucking their tongues and shaking their heads as Mary was smacked down in the hallway. Not a door was opened. Not a word was said. Not a single finger dialed one phone to call the police. Soon the mutual screaming and accusing voices stopped, a door slammed shut, and we all slipped into our beds to get in some much needed reflection as we stared wide eyed at our sensibly white ceilings, vowing "NEXT time things would be different."

I believe that was strike three in the fun filled game of Karma.

FOUR

Just like everything else in our little corner of the world, the night of great shame was never discussed. We all went about our business like nothing had ever happened, but deep inside, I knew it had affected everyone that had been a part of it. I knew this by the way the subject and subjects were so painstakingly avoided. As for myself, I know that I was much closer to Mary after that. I felt guilty as hell and horrible for her, but more than that, I felt horrible for the kids. In the days to follow, their father showed more and more signs of full-blown alcoholism that culminated in his oldest son finding him sitting on the curb in a nearby parking lot puking his guts out.

It was about that time that Mary stopped by my place one afternoon while the kids were in school and her husband was a work. I knew what she wanted, so I gave it to her. We didn't make love because that would imply emotion was involved. We didn't fuck because that would imply sexual gratification. We were just together, and right after that, I was filled with an overwhelming sense of sadness.

Unfortunately, I didn't know myself back then as well as I do now, and I had no earthly concept of the human mind and its capabilities. That one single act would make me feel as though I *owed* Mary something. I couldn't just bang her then walk away; I was emotionally tied to her now.

I would realize years later that she had known this all along.

I would later find out that she had seen a paystub of mine sitting on my table and she knew that I could be her ticket out of shit city. With the simplicity of that one physical act between us, she knew she would be able to manipulate me in any direction she wanted to.

In the years to come, I would allow myself to believe, possibly for self-preservation that I had been doing the responsible thing for her and her children. I now realize that I was simply being manipulated by someone that had everything to gain and nothing to lose.

FIVE

To be forthright here, the events of the next several weeks are still a blur. I spent all my time at home giving Mary the widest berth I possibly could. She, on the other hand spent as much time playing grab ass with me as she could, no matter who was standing there, including her husband or her kids.

I felt bad for the kids because they went on about their life like nothing was happening. That tore me apart. It was like watching a documentary on kids in war torn parts of Africa that had seen so much that they idly played in the street right next to a recently beheaded body as though it wasn't even there. But in my emotionally underdeveloped ignorance, at the time I never thought that they might be acting like this because I *wasn't* Mary's first extracurricular activity and they had been witnessing this for their entire life. Many years later, as I connected the dots, I would realize that neither parent had any idea how to keep their respective genitals in their pants, and this life that looked like a perpetual roving episode of *Cops* was just another day for them.

Then one day, out of the clear blue sky, Mary's kids started calling me dad. Not only should I have seen the handwriting on the

28

wall, but it should have been punching the living shit out of me and screaming, "Wake up idiot!"

They never called me that in front of their father, and they always called me that in front of their mother. Every time that happened, Mary would smile at me like "isn't that the cutest thing you ever saw?"

As I look back, I was actually surprised when Mary came up to my apartment to tell me she had told her husband to pack his crap and hit the road. We were standing in my living room, and as I looked down to the sidewalk there was the object of our conversation walking out to his car with a box full of *stuff* glaring up at me like he would like nothing better than to come upstairs and stomp the hell out of me right then and there.

"Why the hell did you do that?" I asked in amazement.

"You made it clear that there would never be a *me and you* as long as he was here," she told me matter-of-factly.

"You and me? I didn't know there was a you and me."

She pointed over to the couch "What the hell did you call that?" indicating the damning incident of coitus preformed on that very spot.

"I didn't see that as a lifelong commitment," I said in complete, unvarnished, surprise.

"What exactly did you see it as?"

"We had sex."

"So you don't want to have anything to do with me?" Her arms were crossed against her chest. She was totally pissed . . . and accusing.

As I look back on that moment, I should have said, "God damned right!" and ran. Instead, I felt as though I had taken advantage of her, led her on, and now I was the reason her life was falling apart.

I felt totally responsible.

I should have known that this woman had never been taken advantage of in her life; she was a survivor. I think about the conniving, main female character in the Movie *Reindeer Games*. "I never fuck the wrong person!" she says to Ben Affleck.

That was Mary.

I was screwed.

* * *

It has been over a year and a half since I've written these few pages. I just couldn't take the emotions anymore. Today I watched The Today Show *and the continuing saga of Rihanna and Chris Brown was the topic of conversation. Meredith Viera and some PHD are talking about domestic violence and how WOMEN should react to it. Then I picked up the Asheville-Citizen Times and saw an article about trends in violence against women. I was pissed . . . . I started to write letters to the editor, and I did write a letter to* The Today Show *. . . . Then I thought, "Fuck it, who gives a shit." I went down to my office in the basement, played a little guitar, read my E-mails, then I started to work on another book idea. In with my other saved documents I saw the file titled* number six. *I opened it and read what I'd written and my eyes filled with tears. "Stop being such a pussy," I chastised myself. "This is the kind of chicken-shit personality that got you in that place to begin with." Then I reminded myself that if I didn't speak for the men living in quiet desperation, who was going to?*

At the same time, I fought back the creeping feeling that it will all be for naught again. I can't let that feeling rule me.

I'm crying again. Oh well . . . .

SIX

I never thought of this until just this minute, but after she tossed her husband out, Mary never even considered getting a job. All three of her kids were in school, and there were a number of women living in the apartment complex that would have been more than happy to watch the kids after they got home. Mary loved to be the victim and her entire motivation of existence was finding the next person who was going to be her provider.

I tried to get the situation in hand after the great banishing-of-the-husband incident. But I realize now that at twenty-six, and coming from a relatively sheltered background, I was playing WAY out of my league. Hell, I'm not sure I was even playing the same sport as everyone else involved. I actually tried to put a stop to the sex thing after that, and I spent copious amounts of time patting myself on the back for turning her advances away as often as I did. Unfortunately, that is not to say that it never happened again. Making matters worse, I allowed my guilt to go unchecked when it came to the kids. Every chance I got I took them to the park, or invited them up to my apartment to paint or watch TV or make something in the kitchen—anything to take their minds off the fact that both of their parents were acting like children as they vied for the pole position to fuck each other over in the court system in the divorce death race.

The more time I spent with the kids, the more I felt bad for what they were going through. Then one fateful day, Mary came up to my place crying because someone had broken into her apartment through a back window and trashed the place. All of the kid's pictures were gone and Mary's clothes were torn up but nothing else was taken, spoke to the fact that the perpetrator was her soon to be ex-husband.

I went down to survey the damage and I was appalled at what I saw. Things were tossed all around the apartment by someone that was either in a drunken rage or someone that was trying to get a point across. Furniture was overturned, broken glass was everywhere, dresser drawers were ripped out, and the contents were flung on the floor. I couldn't begin to believe that any *normal* person could have done this to someone they knew, let alone someone that they supposedly loved at one time. Then I realized that he hadn't just done this to Mary, he had done this to his kids as well, with no apparent consideration to how they would feel when they saw it.

Little did I know, these two people completely deserved each other. Now when I watch *Cops* and I see some street circus drunks yelling at each other in front of their mobile home, I think, "Hey, I know people just like that, and this is entertainment for them."

My need to be the great protector and fixer of all things kicked into high gear. I told Mary that she needed to leave the apartment just like it was, and move her and the kinds into my place.

And that, as the saying goes, was all she wrote.

SEVEN

My parents had met Mary and the kids; in fact, I had loaded up the brood on two different occasions and hauled them over to my parents' house for lunch. Mom tolerated the kids . . . they both hated Mary. On more than one occasion, my father and I had discussions about my relationship with Mary and the kids. In very intricate detail, dad explained to me that I would always be the odd man out with the family, and no matter what I ever did the dynamic would always be her, the kids and their father—then her and I. As it turned out, he couldn't have been more wrong.

The kids instantly started referring to me as Dad in front of everyone. In fact, I spent more than a little time explaining to them that, while I appreciated the sentiment, they already had a father and that was who he would always be. Their real dad wasn't doing anything to help me out. He spent as much time as he could being drunk and acting like an asshole. The kids turned from him and clung to me, and Mary did everything she could to promote the insanity. The kids even started using my last name in school, providing more than one confusing incident. Mary told everybody she would meet that they were my kids, and I would shyly retreat from the knowing stares as the audience did math in their head indicating that I would have had them when I was still at least in high school, more like Jr. High.

The knowledge of these incidents did nothing to dissuade the feelings of my family. So, to prove I was not nearly mature enough to handle this situation, the more they protested, the more I dug in my heels. Finally, my father told me that there was no way he would ever acknowledge those kids as his grandkids. In retrospect, after seeing how he handled his real grandkids later on in life, they were probably better off not ever getting their hopes up for a family portrait.

The grand finale came one day when dad and I were having another in a long line of heated arguments about Mary.

"Just don't ever tell me that you're thinking about marrying that woman," he said.

"Actually, that's exactly what I'm going to do," I said.

"Son of a bitch," was his thoughtful reply. He threw up his hands and walked away.

That was the last time I would see him or my mother for eleven years.

Mary and I had moved into a townhouse that was big enough to hold my new family of five comfortably, and the house did a wonderful job of eating up nearly every dollar I made. Whatever the townhouse didn't wipe out, Mary neatly polished off, spending like a drunken sailor in the Philippines. I had never been broke before, and now not only was I living from check to check, I had a family that needed to be provided for.

Most of the townhouse was furnished with odds and ends that my parents had taken out of storage in their garage and given me when I got my first apartment. So, just to help out with my instant family, my brother, at the direction of my father showed up at the money pit we called home with his pickup truck.

"What's up?" I asked.

"Dad sent me over to pick up all of their furniture," he told me.

"Really, why didn't he just use his own truck and come to get it himself?" I was pissed, but I was trying not to take it out on my brother.

"Look," he said, "I don't know what he's thinking and I don't want to get in the middle of this thing. Let's just load this crap up and I'll take it home".

So that's exactly what we did. We jammed half of my home into his truck and he drove off to put it all back in my parent's garage. I wouldn't see *him* for another eleven years either. Now I had three kids, a wife, a half-empty townhouse that I couldn't afford, no money, and no emotional support system.

Eventually, I would come to look back on these as the *good* years with Mary.

EIGHT

I realize now that Mary immediately started the long, laborious process of controlling me right from the beginning. No one could have told me what was going on because I was living too close to it, and they weren't. After all, I was no kid for Christ's sake. I was twenty-six years old, I had been halfway around the world in the Navy before I was twenty, and I had already been married once. I knew what was what with my life.

Mary used every available opportunity to carefully explain to me that my family was made up of a bunch of pricks that only wanted to hurt her and keep us apart. Since my parents had broken off all contact with me, I was only getting one side of the story. However, to be completely honest, I doubt I would have listened anyway. It was taking everything I had to keep up with a new wife who was constantly in court over the kids. I had bills mounting up so fast I needed wings to stay above them, and three kids each with personality issues stemming from a shitty relationship. I was losing ground fast and taking on water.

However, the water wasn't rising fast enough for Mary. I came home from work one day to find Mary standing in the middle of the living room with a look on her face that the British could have used at Bunker Hill. Several years before I had met her, she had had a hysterectomy after a miscarriage which created a chemical imbalance. This malady would cause the area around her mouth to turn interesting shades of blue and green whenever she was upset. When I got home that day, her face looked like a cross between a Jackson Pollack and Picasso's blue period.

Apparently she had, for some reason that is not clear over twenty-five years later, called my mother and, wonder of wonders they got into a screaming match. As the story goes, non-flattering names and epithets were exchanged with unbridled glee and phones were slammed down on reinforced plastic receivers. Then, for the cherry on top of this maniacal Dolce De Leche from hell, my father called Mary back and, well, who knows what the hell was really said, but rest assured, pirates docking Queen Ann's Revenge in a gale would have sounded like a Savannah finishing school social compared to what these two said to each other.

I called my father and read him the riot act . . . whatever that means, and he and I had some pretty hate-filled words cast about between us, both in the name of protecting our womenfolk. I

41

immediately came away from that call with mixed emotions. On one hand, I felt good that I had stood up to my father, and stood behind my wife. I felt as though that was the right thing to do. On the other hand, a lot of what dad and I had just finished screaming at each other about, and what Mary told me she had said and done didn't add up. After all these years, I finally realized that I was caught in the middle of two sociopaths who only were interested in winning the argument. Facts were simply something to gloss over as they verbally bludgeoned their way to victory.

After I got off the phone, as I was reflecting on my new found independence and wallowing in the wadi of adulthood, Mary jumped on me like a starving Lion on a crippled fawn.

"WHAT THE FUCK WAS THAT?" she was screaming in my face as she pointed at the phone. Spittle flew from her Technicolor lips, and her lower jaw quivered in anger.

"I uh, I told him off," I said as I tried to figure out what just happened. I mean I had just called my father a fucking asshole in her defense and I thought that was pretty significant.

"DIDN'T YOU HEAR THE THINGS THAT I TOLD YOU HE SAID TO ME?"

"Yeah sweetheart I did," I said defensively, "and that's why I jumped his ass like that."

The more the back and forth went on the more pissed off I got. Mary was clearly unreasonable, and I was going to try to sway her over to my way of thinking.

The yelling lasted for the rest of the day, on into the night nonstop, and ended the next morning when I left, sleepless, for work as she yelled through the door that if I gave a shit about her I wouldn't leave until I fixed the problem. To be honest, I had no idea what the hell the problem really was. I mean in the beginning I understood it, she was pissed that I hadn't been more forceful with my father, but after that issue had been beaten to death, things kind of went downhill.

During the fight I had apologized right off the bat for not supporting her in a way that made her feel like I was on her side. Then she was mad because it wasn't a matter of whose *side* I was on, and that if I thought it was a matter of *sides* then that just proved what a child I was. I told her I didn't get it, and she told me that just showed how much I didn't care about her. In her mind, if I didn't get it, then she wasn't going to explain it to me.

While I was trying to wrap my head around this line of thinking, she started yelling about things that had happened between us that I didn't even *realize* had happened. Apparently, while she was married, and I had no idea how she felt about me, I had another girl friend, and in her mind, I would rub her nose in that as much as I could. I didn't even know what she was talking about, other than the fact that I did indeed have a girl friend at that time, but Mary was supposedly happily married. How the hell was I supposed to know how she felt? In fact, I had broken up with that particular girlfriend before anything had ever happened between Mary and me. That was when I made the first major mistake in our short marriage: I tried to defend myself with logic.

After an entire night of having every single thing that I had ever done to her, real or imagined, screamed into my face, I went to work and reflected on the entire fight. None of it made any sense, and I struggled with trying to get a handle on what the real trigger must have been. We had gone over, in painful detail, nearly every minute of our few years together and none of it offered a glimmer of understanding into what had started an eighteen-hour diatribe. So I decided to apologize one more time as soon as I got home. I was

44

certain that an apology would fix everything as long as I was sincere.

Even now I amazed at just how full of shit I can be.

* * *

Okay, so there goes another year, plus some change. I've done a lot in that time; even my address has changed to another state. Life continues to be better than I hoped it ever would be and still, last night, I had another dream about being trapped in that horrible relationship with a crazy person, unable to get out. It has been over seventeen years since I ran away, and I still have the memories of those unlivable times roll over me as I sleep, like a quilt filled with ice water. Even with all of that, I know that there are hundreds, possibly more, men out there who are currently living the same life I did, and they are certain that there is no way out. Just as they're certain that they are the only guys pussy enough to let themselves get caught up in this.

I continue only for them . . .

Jesus, I've only written 26 pages.

NINE

When I got home, the kids were gone someplace and Mary was laying on the couch with all the melodrama of a Catholic painting of the Virgin Mother at the crucifixion. I could see even after the rough day I just had at work that this conversation was going to be an undertaking that would make Sisyphus cringe.

"Hey," I started out easy so I could work up to the big stuff. "How are you feeling?" I walked over to the couch and sat down next to her. "Look," I said, "I'm sorry about everything that happened yesterday. You were right. I didn't defend you the way that I should have and I can promise you that it will never happen again."

"No," She said moodily, staring off at the ceiling still holding her Madonna like expression . . . allowing false hope to seep into my feeble mind. "It's my fault, I should have known better. I'm such an idiot."

"No, you're not." I should have felt the hook in my lip right there. "What could you have possibly been an idiot about?"

"I should have known that I could never *help* you the way that I wanted to." She looked up at me. "The way that you need me

46

to."

"What do you mean?" I really was uncomfortable with where this was going.

"There's something about you that I've known ever since we met each other. Sometimes when I look at you, I can't even see your eyes. All I can see are dark holes in your face. There's something in there that I know if I do things right, I can fix it. I just need you to help me."

At this point I still had enough semblance of self to think, *"What the fuck?"* but I was determined to fix things between us and get on with providing for her and her kids. I had already been a failure at one marriage, and I knew I could do this.

"Help you how?" I asked naively.

"You have to admit that you have a problem before you can ever begin to fix it," she said pointedly, "and you aren't even close to admitting it."

"Well," I said smiling. "I know that I have a ton of faults, but which one are we talking about, specifically."

She came off the couch like she was blown off it with an overloaded C-4 charge. I still don't know how she got past me without even touching me. That was the first time I noticed her vampire-like qualities.

"How is this funny to you, asshole?" She yelled. Madonna was clearly gone and Satan was in the house. "That's what has been our problem right from the beginning: you and that fucked up sense of humor of yours. How is this funny? How is any of this," she made a sweeping gesture around the unaffordable townhouse half full of furniture, "funny?"

"Your right, your right, I was only—"

"That's right, you're always *only* about something! First it was the never-ending stream of girlfriends you had parading in and out of your apartment right in front of my face! How was I supposed to feel about that? AND you were married before! I want to think that I'm the only person that has ever seen you naked, that I'm the only one that you've ever been with, and you can't even give me that!"

Even as I write this, I am amazed at my stupidity . . . "But you were married before too, sweetheart, and you have three kids," I said gently. How could logic hurt?

Three. Two. One. We have lift off, with immediate first stage

48

separation.

What's that we're seeing now, Wally?

Well, Walter, that would be the phosphorescent explosion that you get as all reason vanishes from the area, and air is sucked back into the void. It's actually very beautiful when viewed from a distance.

Yes it is, Wally. Yes it is. Go baby go!

"Don't you even start that shit with me," she spewed within a fraction of an inch from my face. "You don't even know what life was like with that piece of crap, and those kids were the only thing that kept me sane." (?) "And every time I'd see you up in that apartment, you'd have a different woman up there doing God knows what! Do you have any idea what that did to me? Do you even give a shit?"

"I was only seeing one person at that time…" I was starting to get pissed off all over again.

"AT THAT TIME! Do you even know what that sounds like? AT THAT TIME!" You make me sick. And worst of all you don't even know what I had to do to get over that."

"I know that those things were hard for you…"

"Hard? Hard? You don't know hard! You know that night you were *sleeping* before you had to go in on the midnight shift, and the complex was having a block party, do you remember that?"

Even though this reference may seem vague to the more sane of you, I knew exactly what she was talking about because *that* night had already been the basis of several fights because she didn't want to go to the party alone, and she was pissed at me for trying to get some sleep before I had to be up all night working.

"Yes," I said, "I remember. I should have gone with you."

"Your damn right you should have. Mike wanted to take me for a ride." He was one of the ass grabbers from the night at the country western bar.

"Did you go?" This was certainly new territory we were covering.

"Of course I did. You obviously didn't care or you would have been there with me."

"Where did he take you?"

"We went and sat at the park in his car."

"Did anything happen?"

"I started to . . . ."

Wait . . . was she going to say what I think she's going to say? We were in a committed relationship when this happened.

"Did you blow this guy?"

"I started to, you asshole, and it's all you fault. How do you think that made me feel? Here I am thinking that I can finally have everything in life I want with the man I love, and I never have to notice another man again. Then there I am with someone else because you're gay and you won't accept it! The only reason I stopped was because Mike said he didn't want it that way and he wanted to take me back and have me in his bed."

I can't even begin to tell you the range of emotions that were screaming around in my head right then. She was blowing, albeit in the initial throws of fellatio apparently, the guy that lived downstairs because I was sleeping . . . and it was my fault . . . because I was . . . gay? Did she just say I was gay? Where the hell did that come from?

"Hey, I'm not gay."

"You see, did you see that?" she said, pleading. "You can't even admit it now. I'm standing here telling you that *I* had to go to someone else so *I* could feel like a woman again, and you're still standing there denying that your *female problem* is because you're

51

covering up the fact that you're gay."

Wait . . . what?

What female problem?

I'm not gay.

What the hell was she talking about?

"I don't have a female problem," I said feeling myself starting to get more pissed and trying to keep it under control so I could work this lunacy out.

"Oh-my-God," she said disgustedly. "Look at you." She made a sweeping gesture at me from head to toe and had a look on her face like she had just found a turd in the punch bowl. "Someone else was taking care of your business, and all you can do is stand there like the pussy you are and defend yourself. What about me? I was the one that had to go to someone else!"

"Okay, let's take this thing one step at a time," I said weakly trying to restore some order.

"ONE STEP AT A FUCKING TIME!" she screamed. "I just told you I fucked the neighbor because you weren't man enough to take care of me and you think you have time to take things one step at a time . . . ." She laughed sarcastically and spit in my general direction.

"Actually, no one had mentioned fucking until now," I thought, but I was pretty certain that this was the wrong time to bring that up.

In my mind, I was trying to step back and take an assessment of where I was. Twenty-six years old, responsible for three kids, in debt up to my narrow ass, and as I saw it, unable to back out of this nightmare.

Not a problem . . . I could fix this.

"Just tell me why you think I'm gay," I said as calmly as I could, "and how that made you go to the park with Mike."

"Oh, my God . . . Oh my God," she kept saying with her now pleading face turned toward the ceiling. "I can't believe I was stupid enough to get involved in this. I can't believe I got mixed up with someone as screwed up as you are."

She looked at me with her arms folded across her chest like she was cold. "I thought I could help you . . . I really did," she said, still pleading. "But you're not even willing to help me a little bit."

I can tell you right now sports' fans that I was playing the fastest game of catch up I've ever played in my life. I couldn't believe that she was, very frankly, telling me that she had cheated on me. I should have simply been angry, but there was something in the helpless way she was telling me that made me see her side and, at least as far as she saw it, I wasn't taking care of her feminine needs so she had to turn to someone else. I instantly began to calculate in my mind exactly what I was going to do to fix this problem.

The fact that it couldn't be fixed never even came close to entering my thoughts.

More importantly, the fact that Mary didn't really want *anything* fixed wasn't even close to any semi-conscious thought that I had ever had. All she wanted was control . . . and she was getting it in spades.

I was being introduced to a form of arguing that I would become all too familiar with over the course of the next eleven years of my life. At some point, the kids came home and the fight just continued like it had some kind of surreal momentum of its own. She attacked; I tried to fend off and back down so the kids didn't have to be a part of this. Then, when I would mention that we shouldn't scream at each other in front of the kids, she would go more ballistic because they were "her god damned kids" in the first place, and she knew what was best for them.

Macaroni was boiled, strained, granulated petroleum disguised as cheese was added, I was berated and ridiculed, the orange kind of cheese mess was consumed by all of them while I was glared at, and their day was discussed. Even during this period insults were seamlessly shot at me.

I truly didn't know if I should shit or shoot myself . . . .

For the rest of the night . . . .

I want to pause here to explain that I don't mean "the rest of the night" in any halfhearted way. I mean: *the sun is up . . . oops there it goes, down below the horizon . . . man it is dark . . . here comes the moon and stars . . . I hear birds singing . . . here comes the sun again . . . there goes the alarm clock, gotta get to work.*

So, for the rest of the night we went back and forth in what I would later realize was a fog of insanity. Mary had watched television, showered, gotten ready for bed, and summarily gone to bed all the while fighting with me. Well, that's not exactly accurate. She was berating me and I was defending myself . . . .

And that's when she started drinking.

Right in the middle of a long string of disconnected wrongs

that I had apparently vested upon her, she stopped talking, walked over to the counter in the kitchen, unscrewed the cap from a bottle of wine that should have said, "You don't have shit so you have to drink this crap" on the label, and she stalked off to the bedroom followed by the appropriate, and very theatrical, slamming of the door.

It never even dawned on me until many years after the fact (okay, I'm a little slow) that she never bothered to lock the door. I know now that this was done so that I could continue to play my part in the continuing saga of "Let's all feed Mary's psychosis!"

I walked into the bedroom after her and she was already slugging down the wine like it was giving life to a dead man. Now, during fights prior to this, when the drinking started I had left her in the bedroom basking in the afterglow of much needed silence. That lasted for about thirty minutes before a drunken lunatic would come flying out of the bedroom door, screeching at me because if I had cared about her at all, I would have stopped her from drinking in the first place.

Off into the bedroom I followed so that I could put plan two into effect.

Stop her from getting drunk.

I walked over to the bedside table and made a grab for the wine bottle "Don't you fucking dare," she hissed as she beat me to the grab and sucked a huge amount of crappy wine right out of the bottle.

I stopped . . . so much for plan two.

"That's the same kind of bullshit he used to pull," she slurred. "Control everything I did. Stop me from doing what I wanted, told me who to talk to and who not to, and who to fuck and who I couldn't."

OK, that was new.

"Wait," I said, "he *made* you have sex with other men?"

That was when she lapsed into convenient drunken mumbling, and talking to people that weren't there about incidents that I had never heard about before. She was talking to her father about the time he had tried to have sex with her, and talking to her older brother about the time when he took her out in a field and showed her his penis, and talking to our current next door neighbor about what a pretentious bitch she was.

That was when she puked all over the bed.

I picked her up off the bed, sat her limply in a chair, changed the bed clothes, put her back in it, and tucked her in.

Now, I don't want to try and pass myself off here as Gandhi or Jesus. I have my faults and plenty of them, but if I'm nothing else, I'm introspective. My previous marriage had lasted all of one year and three months. We had issues, but nothing that couldn't have been overcome with some conversation and reasoning. In fact, the biggest problem that we had was that we were both twenty-three, a touch selfish, and had no idea how to live with another person in our lives. Naturally I went to my father for guidance and he, very thoughtfully advised me, "Dump that bitch. I wouldn't put up with her shit for a minute."

So I did.

Now, in this relationship there was nothing I wouldn't do to make things right. Every time I wanted to tell Mary to shut the fuck up and get some psychiatric help I checked myself. Every time I wanted to just walk away from the whole mess I checked myself. Eventually that self-control would work wonders for me.

TEN

Through this entire hillbilly hullabaloo, Mary was going through her divorce . . . so . . . believe it or not, we weren't even married at this point. I know that as I look back on this mess, I easily could have walked away from the whole sordid episode at any time I wanted. I also realize that Mary knew this, and consequently she kept her real craziness in semi-check while she was working overtime to control me so that I wouldn't leave.

Plans were being made from the proverbial "get go" for me to make an honest woman out of her as soon as her divorce was final. As I said before, money was leaving my bank account so fast it made a whooshing sound that could be heard for miles, so naturally Mary wanted the most expensive wedding dress she could find . . . white of course . . . and new clothes for all three of the kids. I won't go over the intricacies of the fight that ensued when I told her I couldn't afford that much because it is almost identical to the one mentioned in the last few chapters. Money was simply the kindling that was used to start the larger bonfire of distress.

No money.

You fucker.

No I'm not.

Yes you are.

You're gay.

No I'm not.

Yes you are.

What about what happened two years ago.

You're right. I was an asshole.

You still are.

I'm sorry.

I'm drunk.

The outcome, which is always the most important part of needless bickering, was Mary very patiently explaining the world of high finance to me. Apparently you get all of the credit that your wallet can possibly hold, and then you run those suckers right straight up to the limit and pay the minimum payment. When you pay the balance down a few hundred dollars you punch it right back up to full again. Of course this flew right in the face of anything that I had ever been taught about fiscal responsibility, but I wanted to give Mary and the kids the things in life they never had. The only way to do that was run up massive amounts of debt and worry about it later. The upside was that Mary offered to take over paying the bills, since she knew what it took to run a household of five.

That sounded good to me.

We were married by the justice of the peace in the local court house. Mary was in an all-white wedding dress so expensive that it should have driven us there, parked itself, then taken us home and made dinner. The boys were in brand new suits that they would only wear once. The girl was in a brand new dress. And I was wearing the only suit I had and a grin that should have come with a blindfold and a cigarette.

Things after that were a nonstop rollercoaster of emotional insanity. I saw a picture of myself during that period the other day and I was amazed that I looked older over twenty years ago than I do now. The kid's father was a total drunken dick. Naturally, he got married almost instantly also, and his new wife had either a kid or kids, I don't remember now. What I do remember is that his new step-family was apparently taking precedence over his real family. Naturally when the kids spent time together, there was a tremendous vying for attention. When my step kids would come back from a visit they would talk about how one of them had gotten in a fight with the extended family and their father had taken the wrong side. This would generate a phone call from Mary to the ex that would always either end up, or start outright, in a screaming match.

At first, I tried to stay out of it and offer emotional support to the kids. In my mind, what they needed was a little stability. Apparently in Mary's mind they needed a champion, and she needed vindication. She and I had more than one go around about my lack of enthusiasm when it came to "slapping a knot in their father's ass." I could only think that any amount of "knot slapping" was going to, at the very least, lead to rolling around in the front yard of someone's house, topped off by a little discussion with the local police in the middle of the night. But the seed had been planted and I knew I was going to have to confront the father, if for no other reason than to keep Mary happy.

Consequently, one night, in the front yard of their fathers' new house, Mary and I were picking the kids up from visitation. The new wife was there, naturally, as well as the new step-kid (or kids) and Mary's oldest boy picked *this* time to be a smart ass to his father. *So*, daddy being the thoughtful type that he was, and bolstered by many, many beers, punched his thirteen-year-old son right in the mouth.

Years later, I would find myself desperately craving the ability to re-enact that scene.

Naturally, I instantly knew that I only had one option here, and it was load the kids up in the car, go home, and notify child protective services.

But that would have made too much sense.

I jumped on the father's back and initiated the backcountry cage match. Clearly everyone involved had been craving this for way too long. A great wailing and gnashing of teeth issued forth from the womenfolk. The kids yelled and jumped out of the way of the two adult males who were making total assholes out of themselves. Dogs barked wildly. Oaths were yelled. Horrible names and accusations were spewed out, and three neon letters kept rolling through my mind's eye.

WTF?

He and I actually pulled ourselves apart after it became obvious that no one else was going to. Mary and I stuffed three yelling kids into our 100% financed used car. Threats were slung around like candy flying out of a piñata. Gravel spit from the tires as

I screamed out of the driveway needlessly fast, and off we went back to our little love nest.

Mission complete.

ELEVEN

I started to take stock of my life up to this point. Mary had gone into overdrive trying to keep me in my place. I didn't realize until decades later, this was all classic abuser mentality. When it looked like my family and I were going to actually make things work, she deftly put the screws to that ever happening, hence the phone call to my father, and an identical one to my sister. The retelling of both of these incidents was greatly modified from reality when they were related to me. Consequently, when I contacted the family member that had apparently been very uncharacteristically horrible to my new wife, I put the finishing touches on never seeing them again, insuring that they would stay out of Mary's way.

Whenever I would relate work stories to Mary about some type of camaraderie between me and my co-workers, Mary would get exasperated because I refused to see that everyone I worked with was a total backstabbing asshole. In fact, any of the men Mary had met that I worked with, according to Mary, had tried to get in her pants. I certainly couldn't go to work and ask any of them about this because naturally they would tell me that it never happened, so I was left to simply take her word for it.

I know that it sounds like Mary told me things and I would simply accept it, but you have to understand the mind of an abuser. These things are calculated very carefully and contain an incredible amount of fore thought and planning. She and I had conversations for *hours* about how she always had my best interest in mind and that she wanted me to be the best person that I could possibly be, and she just wanted me to understand that I was better than all of the people I worked with, and that they were jealous of the things we had together.

Naturally by this time, I was pretty much cut off from the rest of reality so I had no normality to gauge things against. The very interesting part to this control struggle was the other end of the spectrum. Every single insecurity I had in my personality was completely exploited by Mary at every opportunity she had. When I was ten or eleven years old, my father, an overly macho bundle of insecurity himself, started to get on me about my weight and the fact that I hated to work out. His new pet name for me was *fat boy,* and he was constantly on my back to be more physically fit.

"Look at yourself," he would say. "You have an ass like a woman. You really need to do something about that."

Apparently the fact that I was already pushing six ft, only weighed 140 lbs and played football were lost on him.

At any rate, my sexuality and weight were always hot button issues with me. When Mary and I were married, I was six ft three and weighed around 170. She had me on a diet constantly. She told me that I was built just like my dad, all gut with chicken legs. She told me that I needed to start taking care of myself and work out. Every opportunity she got, she would point men out to me that she thought were attractive and tell me that if I cared about her at all, I would work on making myself look like that.

Conversely, Mary was the most jealous person that I had ever before, or since, seen. In the beginning, I took each incident individually and was unable, or unwilling to connect the dots. Mary's problem with my mother seemingly was connected to the problem she had with my father and the rest of my family, same for my sister, and in my defense, this all made sense if you considered the openly hostile posture my mother and father had taken against Mary in the beginning of our relationship. I never even began to consider the truth that Mary's problem with them was simply because they were women.

Mary would get unbelievably pissed off if I talked to a waitress in a restaurant and I could understand why she might feel this way because I had always been an outgoing kind of a person, so I tried to tone that down. When my 'toning it down' wasn't enough, I tried to keep any conversation between me and any female staff to a minimum. After all, that person meant nothing to me and I was trying to build a relationship with my wife. If she had a problem with me being friendly to waitresses then I would stop doing that and all would be right with our world. When 'keeping it to a minimum' wasn't good enough, then I eventually became outwardly hostile to female service people that I would be forced to come in contact with in public.

The thing that I didn't anticipate was Mary's next move. Apparently my being a prick to total strangers was causing her to be uncomfortable, so every time we would encounter a woman in public and I was forced to actually speak to them, as clipped and unemotionally as I possibly could, Mary would fall into a deep, face-color-changing funk. When we would get home, without fail, she would start to berate me because the only reason I had to act like an asshole to women was because I couldn't control myself around

69

them. I had to be trying to get them in bed or I would have to be a total jerk to them. If I really cared about her, I would find a happy medium in the way I handled females, and we could get on living our newly happy life.

Every time I got into another situation involving a woman, at a restaurant, mall store, fast food place, toll booth, or any place else—and it happened all the time because Mary didn't do anything by herself. She would wait until I got home and we would all go together—I would find myself working my ass off to make sure that NOTHING happened to make Mary feel insecure. This was just the first in a long line of issues that I thought, "this is no big deal. If my wife has a problem with it, then I'll just change it for the sake of our marriage and all will be well."

At the apex of this jealousy sky rocket, and several more years into our marital bliss . . . long after I had gotten used to having the shit beaten out of me . . . we were at the pickup window of a Burger King. I had spit the order into the feminine sounding speaker as hatefully as I could, following that up with the obligatory "ignorant bitch" as I drove around to pick up our order. When I paid the innocent woman at the window, she reached out and put her left hand under mine to avoid spilling any change and her finger tips pressed into the palm of my hand as she gave my money.

I could feel the heat from Mary's stare on the back of my head and I really had no idea what I had done wrong.

"Did she touch you?" Mary asked like she was asking if I thought it might rain this evening.

"Ummm, what?" I asked, truly not knowing what she was talking about, but fully understanding that I was in deep shit.

"Did *you let* that whore in the drive thru touch you?"

"Ah, I didn't let her do anything—"

SLAM! She drove my head into the side window of the car. "If you didn't care enough about me to stop her, then you let her!"

Of course there was a lot of yelling and violence as I tried to drive us home, but the biggest thing that I got out of that forty straight hours of fighting was a lesson in how to keep a woman from actually getting girl cooties on me when I went through a drive thru. First, ALWAYS keep a ton of change in my car. Second, pay attention to what the exact amount is going to be when you pay, and last, but by no means least, take the paper money and fold it in half long ways, put the change in the fold, fold it in half *again* the other

71

way, and hold on to the end when I pass it through the window. I did that for so long, and a few other insane things that I'll get into later, that I still find myself starting to do it seventeen years after the fact.

Eventually, this psychosis wormed its way into every facet of our lives. I knew that Mary had a giant problem with me seeing any type of nudity in the movies. We had had more than one knockdown drag out over that. I figured that I would give it one more try with what I thought HAD to be a female free movie, and we went to see "Platoon". Now I know what you're thinking, "Who was the woman in platoon? Oh yeah the rape scene . . . or evacuating the village."

Not so.

On the way home from the theater I was feeling pretty good about myself. I had successfully taken Mary out to the movies and completely avoided the "woman" issue. What I couldn't explain was the blue green haze covering her face that I could even see in the dark car.

"So what did you think?" I asked.

"What did YOU think?" she said.

"Oh shit!" I thought. "I liked it," I said.

"I bet you did," came the dark reply.

"What's the matter sweetheart?" I asked

"If you gave a shit about me you'd already know."

She was pissed about the scene when Bunny and Junior are talking in the troop area about the evils of smoking grass. Whenever the camera goes back to the actor lying on the cot, there is a pin up on the wall behind him. All of "Platoon" had been reduced to that one small area of that one scene. That was the last movie I saw for the next ten years. If that caused her any type of problem then I didn't need to watch movies. Nothing was more important than fixing my marriage and making Mary happy.

The next form of media to bite the dust was TV and that was due to "Dallas". Mary loved that program and "Knots Landing". One day I made an off handed comment in response to her telling me about an episode of one show or another. I said that I thought the women in Knots Landing were more realistic than the ones in Dallas. I don't even need to tell you how much crap hit how big of a fan after that.

Bye-bye, TV.

Radio and music were next to go, followed by print media.

Oddly enough, none of that fixed Mary's insecurity.

So there I was: everything that came out of my mouth and every action that I took made my wife know just how much I don't care. I was raising three kids, one of which had no idea how to stay out trouble in school. I was up to my eyeballs in debt that I could never possibly hope to pay off. My family had turned their back on me and I didn't see any way out of this nightmare.

I saw my life at this point as unchangeably hopeless.

However I was worth about half a million dollars dead.

One night, I was sitting at the dining room table after Mary and the kids went up to bed. Work that day had been a bitch. The woman that lived across the street had come over to use our phone because hers didn't work and one of the kids let her in. Even though I hadn't even acknowledged her presence, Mary wanted to know how long I had been cheating on her with this woman. Naturally, there had been a long drawn out fight and plenty of insane accusations thrown around.

The fight was either over now or had subsided for a few minutes. My gun was lying on the table in front of me. I know I put it there and I know what my intension was, but I didn't actually remember the events that got it loaded and shoved into my mouth. I didn't have any emotional feeling attached to the moment even when I pulled the trigger and it refused to budge.

I hadn't pulled the slide back to chamber a round.

I remember thinking, "Huh, I'll be damned."

I jacked a round into the chamber and was sticking the barrel back in my mouth.

"Are you coming up to bed or are you going to sit down there all night thinking about your girlfriend?" it was Mary calling down the stairs.

"Fuck it," I thought. I didn't even care enough to pull the trigger anymore.

I went upstairs and went to bed instead of finally putting an end to everything.

* * *

Okay, that was harder than I had expected. I hadn't thought about the feeling of feeling nothing at all for a long time. The amazing part is that I just finished typing this, got up went out to see the horses for a little while, and joked with my wife for a few minutes. Inside my head there is someone curled up in the corner with his eyes closed just wishing that the world would go away.

Whoever said that writing your feelings down is good therapy is a total   *asshole.*

TWELVE

Life at that point had turned into one long line of pushing myself from one day to the next . . . and little did I know that things hadn't even gotten bad yet.

I realized that I was going to have to do something to insure that there was more money coming into the household. Working another job was pretty much out of the question because of my rotating shift work. So I had an opportunity to move to a bigger city and a larger facility than the one that I was working in at the time. The downside would be that the stress at the new job would be crushing compared to the place where I was currently. At any rate, that was my problem. At least we would have more money.

As in most facilities, right after I reported in, I was invited to bring my wife in so she could meet the people I worked with. Had I had anything to say about this, I would have insured that this trip never took place. But this place I was working in had mailed the invitation to my home. Even though there were a lot of women working there, I had gone out of my way to be a total turd to them;

77

just in case I saw one of them on the street, she wouldn't make the mistake of saying hello to me. I was sure that Mary being around the people that I worked with could go no place good.

Sometimes I get tired of being right all the time.

Mary and I walked into the facility and as soon as we got out of the elevator there were about three secretaries standing around in the hallway. Apparently, I had been a big enough jerk and I breathed a huge sigh of relief when they completely ignored us. Just the same, a cloud fell over Mary's face and I knew that I was in for it when I got home. I just didn't know what the fuel was for this particular fire. But I was wrong about one thing. It started as soon as we got into the *car* to go home.

"What's the matter?" I asked.

"Why am I not surprised that you would have to ask me that?" she said sullenly.

"I'm really sorry—"

"Boy, that's no shit."

"Honestly, sweetheart I—"

"Honestly? Really! You have the balls to sit there and start anything that you have to say to me with *honestly*?"

78

"I certainly haven't lied to you about anything."

"I sure that you *certainly* believe you haven't, but that just proves how much my life sucks, and how much the only thing you give two shits about is yourself."

"So what the hell did I do now?!" There was still too much of a semblance of *me* left, and I didn't have the presence of mind to keep my mouth shut no matter what amount of hatred and abuse was being spit in my face.

I was just pulling onto the interstate and POW she hit me right in the ribcage. I was startled because she had never done that before.

"Hey!" I said as I rubbed my side.

"Oh yeah, right," she screamed "protect yourself, you pussy. I'm the one that always gets jacked around by you and you have the balls to think about yourself first. What about me, you worthless prick? What about Me! I walk in that facility and the first thing that I see is your picture hanging on the wall above all of those whores you work with. Which one took it? Did you fuck her afterwards? You did, didn't you, you piece of shit!"

POW, another shot in the side. I didn't touch it that time. I'm a quick study.

"What picture are you talking about?" I really didn't know.

"Of course you don't know, you asshole. You wouldn't"

Then it hit me, (no pun intended). In the hallway, as soon as you got out of the elevator, management had put everyone's photo up on the wall with their names underneath. We had been getting a lot of new people there and they thought it would be a good idea to put everyone's photo up so we would know who each other were. The icing on the cake was that my photo was hung up right next to one of the women that worked there.

Needless to say, that funfest lasted the rest of the day and long into the night. The thing that set it apart from the endless string of other insane days and nights were two things. First, once we got home Mary took her first full on swing at me. Instinctively I leaned back out of the way. That really pissed her off, and she started ripping my clothes out of the closet and tossing them out the front door of our apartment unto the wet grass.

"Get out!" she screamed at me "All you give a shit about is protecting yourself. You couldn't care less about me, so get your shit, and get the fuck out!"

I was busy as a cat covering up crap trying to defuse this situation. We lived in a real rough part of town and the cops were going to be there any minute if this lunacy didn't either stop or move back into the house.

I was standing there trying to reason with her, and the more I tried to be rational the more she lost her mind. Finally, she stalked back into the house grabbed the car keys, stalked back out past me, fired up the car, and left a fairly large portion of the tires and about twenty dollars worth of gas that had been quickly converted to carbon monoxide in the parking lot.

A normal person would have gone in the house and gone to bed, but I knew that she was going to be right back, and if she caught me sleeping I wasn't sure what she was capable of now that we were obviously into the hitting phase.

A few hours later, the front door opened revealing the return of the Madonna, completely converted to consummate victim sporting slumped shoulders and pitiful eyes.

"I was worried about you," I said.

"Don't bother."

I was relieved that we were at least out of the high octane

whacked out phase. At least this current manifestation would talk to me.

"I always care about you," I said. We had only been married a little more than three years and already these words were starting to sound hollow in my head.

"You have a real shitty way of showing it," she said as she slumped down on the sofa. I remember that I felt guilty as I stole a glance at the clock. It was about two in the morning and I had the six to two day shift in a few more hours. Oh well, I had gotten pretty good at running on fumes with sleep deprivation.

After Mary had flung herself, and our only mode of overly financed transportation out of the parking lot, she drove up past the airport and onto the interstate. About two miles down the road, she saw a sign for Chicago (still about 280 miles down the road) and she thought she had driven all of the way there. That scared her so she turned around and came home. For the rest of that night we sat in the living room and calmly talked about what a piece of crap I was, how I had destroyed her life and how she hated herself for bringing her kids into a screwed up mess like this.

I was ecstatic. We were actually talking.

We had moved from full on crazy to the "woe is me" part, and all I had to do was agree with her that I was, for all practical purposes, worthless, and she was an overly amazing woman that trudged through life cleaning up my shit and dealing with my screwed up problems. I knew even as I heard the alarm clock go off in the upstairs bedroom signaling the fact that I was soon going to have to get a shower and try to be on time for work, that at some time in the future I was going to have eat every single word that I agreed with that night, and even some words that never passed my lips that had been made up for the sake of drama.

Even if she had no sense of geography, Mary certainly made up for that with an awesome memory. Sometimes her memory was so good that she was able to remember things that didn't even happen . . . with surprising clarity. She had an exact idea of what she wanted her life to be like. The fact that this plan would change with whatever personality would manifest itself at the time was irrelevant to the person who was supposed to be supplying that life to her. I was simply supposed to know which Mary was in the room at the time and   deal   accordingly.

THIRTEEN

Six months, one apparent murder next door, one break in where the only thing stolen were all of my firearms, and countless melodramatic scenes later, Mary and I completed the domestic violence motif by moving into a doublewide mobile home in a very nice trailer park out in the middle of nowhere. The oldest boy was pretty much in perpetual trouble with the park management. Mary wanted what she wanted, and it was up to me to make it happen, and work . . . well, let's just say that in a chosen profession that ranked in the top three for alcoholism, drug dependency, divorce, and suicide, I was now in the big time, and treading water as fast as my little legs would carry me.

Shortly after the Photo incident at work, I witnessed a United DC-8 crash on the airport killing everyone aboard. I saw an opportunity to make sure that my personal life and work life never touched each other ever again. I told Mary that security at the facility was being tightened up while the NTSB (National Transportation Safety Board) investigated the crash and no one was allowed to go there if they didn't have a security clearance. As far as she knew, that investigation lasted three years, and was still going on when we left for another facility.

During that time, I continued to work overtime, trying to be a total prick at work so anyone I met from there in public would stay away and not do anything to trigger another incident with Mary. She was already convinced that since I got thirty minutes for lunch and a fifteen minute break every two hours, I was using that time to get laid. Mary had effectively been very successful at domestic violence 101. I was now totally cut off from family, outside friends, and co-workers. My entire world consisted of her and the kids.

The guy that lived next door to us in the mobile home park was single, and seemed to be friendly enough. To be honest, it was good to have someone living next to me that didn't have a wife or a girlfriend I would be forced to treat like shit. We didn't spend much time together but every once in a while he would walk past the house while I was outside working in the yard and we would exchange pleasantries. It was like a breath of fresh air.

Then, out of the clear blue sky blue-green faced Mary shows up and during an out of control, carnie ride, yelling match she says—completely off hand—that if she had still been married to her ex-husband, she would have already slept with the guy next door. I know that I should have been pretty much numb to whacked- out, off the wall crap, but this really caught me off guard. I asked her why the hell she would say that, and I wanted to know if he had made any advances towards her. That question brought an avalanche of insults and accusations. I realize now that this, although it seems crazy to the casual observer, was carefully thought out by Mary, just as it is any abuser. It's the valuable tool of misdirection. As soon as things start to get to close to placing the blame where it should be, the conversation is redirected back at the victim.

"If I end up in bed with him, I'll never forgive you," Mary screamed into my face.

"How the hell am I supposed to keep you from banging the guy next door?" I yelled back.

Mary's right cross caught me unrepentantly under my left temple. I was surprised that instinctively I wanted to beat the dog shit out of her. But I also was knew that she was right, (the conditioning was nearly complete), all I had to do was *love* her enough and show her how much she meant to me and naturally no one else would be able to work their way into our life . . . or her bed.

I shook the cob webs out of my head and fought the urge to

rub the side of my face. I knew that would really piss her off because I was taking care of myself and not thinking about how I made her feel bad when she had to hit me.

"How do you think that makes me feel, you self-centered asshole?" she yelled at me with pleading eyes. "After everything that I had to do when I was married before, I thought that I would never have to notice another man again. I thought that it would always only be you, and now thanks to your *gay* problem and all of your kissing other women's asses, I have to worry about sleeping with the next door neighbor."

I knew that this was nuts. If Mary didn't want to sleep with the guy next door she didn't have to, no matter what I did or didn't do, but my mind was too far gone to make that connection. I also knew that in Mary's mind, this was the farthest thing from reality. I had the responsibility of making things right for her, and I was, if nothing else, a fixer. I knew that I could do this for her and everything would be fine. Just one more hurdle, one more thing for me to make a concession on, one more burden for me to shoulder. I could do this. That would take away any other reason Mary had to hit me. She would be happy. Little animated blue birds would ride on my shoulder and sing in my ear and the sun would come up in a Technicolor blast that would blind lesser men.

Just one more thing I had to change . . . one more thing…that's all . . .

About this same time, Mary bought a membership at a local gym, and whenever she wasn't at home watching QVC, or writing country western songs about what a piece of crap I was, or how hard her life had been, she was at the gym supposedly working out. This was great for me because it seemed to keep her happy. Unfortunately, she only went there while I was at work. She told me, during another argument, that this was a strain on her personal life as well because she knew that she had to keep an eye on me whenever I was home. Even though I had never given her any reason to think this way, she said she couldn't trust me by myself.

One day during a lull in marital combat Mary was telling me about a new friend she had at the gym. *He* was well built, attractive, sensitive, and insecure about his looks. According to Mary, they spent most of the time they were at the gym together sitting in the hot tub talking about day's events, hopes, dreams, and life in general. I was about four years into my indoctrination and I was trying to juggle an out of control pre-teen, a neighbor that I was desperately trying . . . somehow . . . to keep out of my wife's pants, and the park manager who was trying to have us and our trailer tossed out of the park. Supposedly, it was due to the deck that I built off our side door, but I was pretty sure it was because Mary had gotten into a fight with him when she took our rent check to the office and she had called him a fat piece of shit. Consequently, Mary's new friend seemed to make her happy, and she constantly assured me that there was nothing between them. She even assured me of that when she was bitching about some woman in the hot tub with them that was clearly coming on to her totally platonic friend. She even assured me that there was nothing going on there when she told me that she saw up the leg of his shorts one day as he got into the tub and he had a huge dick.

To the guy that had a gun sticking in his mouth just a year or so before, the size of some other guy's dick was nothing to get cranked up about.

So I was kind of surprised when I woke up in the middle of the night, Mary gone, and a note left on her pillow. "I have to go and work some things out with _____," it read. "Don't worry, everything will be alright."

I guess there had been an issue in the hot tub that needed immediate action.

No gentle reader...it never occurred to me that this was the exact same thing she had said to husband #1 when she came up to "work something out" with me so many years before.

I got out of bed and sat in the dark with the note, wondering where all of this was going to go. Obviously I had failed in the keeping Mary's genitals at home department, no matter what the note said. I sat there until the early morning glow of a Midwest sunrise started to give muted color to the room. I've grown to hate that time of day. The kids got up and I got them ready for school. No one asked where mommy was because I got them ready for school every morning when I didn't have a day shift so Mary could sleep in after a hard day of not screwing the neighbor or sitting in a hot tub. So I didn't mention the fact that mommy was among the missing.

About an hour after the kids left to catch the school bus, our car pulled into the parking space across the street. Mary had the put on the Madonna look as she came in the house. I asked her what happened and where she went. I guess I fully expected a full on brawl, or at least a screaming match. In retrospect I think that I expected that because I knew I could handle something like that. Infidelity was going to be just one more thing on an already overflowing plate. I honestly didn't care about much anymore and I was just sleepwalking through my life, praying for a car accident or a quick heart attack so this would all be over.

What I got was a woman sitting in front of me telling me about the problems of her relationship with her gym partner. This was new, but anything resembling love for Mary had long ago left the building. Now I was just trying to do the right thing for a woman and three kids that I had wrested from the (in Mary's convoluted retrospect) loving arms of a husband and provider, and the father of her children—well two of them anyway. Apparently my predecessor wasn't any better than me in fighting off the competition.

As the story goes, Mary was awake and couldn't sleep because she wanted to "get things straight" between her and gym guy. What needed to get straightened out isn't really clear to this day. Anyhow, she left me my note and drove out to the warehouse where this guy worked the midnight shift. I guess he was surprised to see her. I know that I sure as hell would have been. He took her out to the parking lot. They got in his pickup truck, and there, amidst the romance of asphalt, parked cars and halogen lights, she asked him if he had ever thought about being with her. He said he had. His penis accidentally slipped into her mouth as he drove her off to a hotel and they spent the rest of the night "being with each other."

But the cherry on top of this little dime-novel story of romance was the fact that Mary couldn't really *enjoy* her time with her new boyfriend because she spent too much time, I guess on her back with her legs in the air, thinking about me.

That last part resonates with me, even to this day. There was no question in my mind that Mary's point was that I had even stolen *the joy of her infidelity*. She was unable to get everything out of the ass slamming she was being given because she was thinking about me. It was not, "I know I screwed you over baby . . . but I was thinking about you the whole time," but instead, "You've even crapped on this in absentia."

As I look back on this, I'm amazed at my emotionless, bovine-like reaction to this mess. I've tried to explain it to a few people, and to a person they have all looked at me like I had three heads while vowing that they would NEVER allow themselves to be in that position. Of course, I was left to think of myself as a weak, poor excuse of a man. Even now as this bile spills off my fingertips, I'm having a hard time dealing with myself for reacting that way. But I was totally sympathetic to Mary's plight, and more than that, I felt totally responsible. I was not only responsible for the fact that there was a late night meeting at a hotel, but moreover, I was responsible for the fact that she really couldn't enjoy herself.

* * *

Right now I'm screaming at myself inside to stop writing this. I know that I'm only opening myself to ridicule. The same ridicule that I've opened myself to in the past from family and friends alike. Right now, I can see the judgmental looks from people that were supposed to mean something to me as I told them what my life had been like. My father told my sister just a few months before he died that I was "one sick fucker" for ever allowing that to happen. If I tried to explain to someone how I got to that point in the first place, I always came across as trying to make it sound okay so that I didn't look so bad. I know right now that I'm trying to get YOU to look at with me with less than disdain.

Jesus Christ, I just want to quit this! Things are just fine when I press all of this into the back of my mind and go on like it never happened. I can play like I'm okay, just like everybody else, like I was never reduced to the emotionless punching bag that I was.

But I can't stop.

I know that I owe it to other men out there who are living the same life I did. I know that I'm not the only one because I've had more than one person relate stories like this to me.

Or maybe I'm full of shit. Maybe I had all of this coming and I was too weak to keep it from happening. I don't know.

But I do know that I'm working my ass off right now to convince you that I had no control over it.

* * *

Mary spent several hours relaying the events of the night before to me and I spent several hours apologizing to her for putting her in that position. Naturally, she told me that it was my responsibility to keep it from happening again, and naturally I took on that responsibility. After all, if I had been more sensitive and caring right from the beginning, we wouldn't be in this place right now.

And my underlying gay issues didn't help. . . .

Of course there was no way that the sexual trysts were going to stop. Mary was getting everything she wanted AND she had a perfect scapegoat for her own guilty feelings. She wasn't doing anything wrong. It was all my fault, and she was begging me to not let it happen again.

I had no idea how much worse it could get and how much lower   I   could   sink.

FOURTEEN

I would eventually learn the hard way that with Mary paying all the bills that I had a very interesting piece of legislation working hard in my favor. I was a federal employee, and the only thing that a business could garnish my wages over was unpaid child support, as long as there was a court order. What they could do, however, was call your place of employment as many times as they wanted to "verify employment." Naturally, when staff received calls like this, they knew exactly why the call was being made, and since we had all signed conduct and discipline papers upon our employment, we all knew that any tawdry conduct unbecoming a federal employ at or away from work was grounds for dismissal.

One day, after I was relieved from a control position, the area manager told me that the facility chief wanted to talk to me in his office. There were only two reasons for the boss to want to talk to me personally. Either I was going to get an award for exemplary service, or I was going to get my ass chewed. I was certain that it wasn't the first because I had fallen from a model employee, to an introverted, preoccupied, just-barely-getting-the-job-done type since

I had Mary in my life. However, I had no idea why I would be getting an ass chewing because I hadn't done anything wrong.

The facility Manager was an old school kind of guy, meaning that he had made his reputation working on the boards then started his climb up the ladder. He still had a worker bee mentality, and the rank and file liked him for it. When I got into his office, the Deputy Manager was sitting there also, and I may not have known why, but the fact that I was in deep shit was obvious. I sat in the chair across from the chief's desk and stood by to receive whatever lumps I had coming and subsequently throw myself on the mercy of the court.

"We received a call from Household Retail Services today verifying your employment," he began. The deputy sat next to him boring an icy hole in the side of my head, with a fixed, judgmental stare.

"Oh," I said blankly. I felt like throwing up. This job was all I ever wanted to do since I was in the seventh grade. From the time I was seventeen years old, I charted out my career all the way to retirement and vowed to let nothing get in my way. Now I was in the big time and a creditor, of all things, was about to take a giant dump on all I had worked for. I could have been more embarrassed, but I don't know how.

"Do you know what that's all about?" he asked flatly.

"Yes sir, I do," I said thinking that honesty might be the best policy but an undue offering of information might not have been the smartest thing at that particular juncture.

"And I assume that you're going to take care of it . . . right?" he asked.

"Yes sir."

"And I'm not going to get any more of these calls . . . am I."

He looked over at the deputy, and they exchanged blank looks that somehow conveyed everything each other needed to know.

"*Holy shit*" I thought "*these guys are telepathic.*"

"Get lost," the chief said.

"Gladly," I said as I stood up . . . then "Look Chief, I really don't know how any of this happened and I'm really sorry, I'll take care of it right now."

He tilted his head toward the door.

I made use of it.

I was mortified. There were two axioms that my mother had

beaten into my head as I grew up, fiscal responsibility, and NEVER do anything half assed. I was in the process of dumping all over the first one, and was following up with number two by letting it seep into my work. I knew that we were so far in debt that we would never be out of it, but I *thought* that all the bills were being paid. The money was definitely going away, and we were definitely living from pay check to pay check, so on the surface it looked to me like the bills were being paid.

I went down to the terminal where there was a bank of payphones, and I called Mary. I was scared to death.

"HRS just called the facility because we owe them money," I said, expecting to hear her be just as mortified as I was.

"So?" she said.

"Why would they call here? Are we behind?"

"Yeah, a little, but so what?"

"So they're calling the facility to collect their money. Have they been calling us?"

"Yeah, the collection agency has."

Holy shit, this thing had gone to collection and I didn't even know it. What happened to the letters, and threats, and . . . . Oh my

God, she got them all and threw them out before I saw them.

"Why didn't you tell me this was going on before it got this far?" I asked.

"Because, I knew that this is exactly what you would do, and I'm trying to run a household here, and put up with your bullshit at the same time. I knew that you would cave in like the little pussy you are, and try to pay these assholes off."

"Yeah I'd try to pay them off." I was angry now, and that was dangerous. "We owe them money that we borrowed in good faith! They're going to take me to court and I'm going to lose my job!"

"We already got a letter saying that they're going to sue us."

I didn't say anything for a while; I had to let that little nugget sink in just a little.

"Did you just say that they're going to sue us?"

"Yeah, so what? You see, this is exactly the kind of bullshit I was talking about. Anybody can say they're going to sue you, it doesn't mean anything. They just go down to the court house and pay the $85 court fee and file the paper work. It doesn't mean that it will even get to court."

How the hell did she know how much the court fees were?

"What else aren't we paying?" I asked flatly. I could feel the resignation of my life going almost totally out of control, and it was going to be one more thing that I was going to shut myself off to, and this clicking roller coaster car wasn't all the way to the top of the first hill yet.

"Listen to me you idiot," she hissed into the phone. "I'm doing everything I can here to make ends meet, and I certainly don't need this crap out of you right now. That job that you're so in love with is one of our biggest problems, and you care more about it that you do me. The day that you finally walk away from it and start doing an honest day's work is going to be the happiest day of my life."

CLICK!

I could feel the receiver being slammed down on the other end of the phone. It sounded a lot like my life spiraling even farther down the crapper.

Naturally HRS sued the hell out of us, well, me actually, and Mary was too "sick" to go to the court date. But at the same time, she knew that she couldn't trust me to go to the courthouse alone because I would "make an ass" out of myself flirting with all the women there, so there I stood in front of the judge as my preteen step daughter looked on, and the court and the HRS lawyer ate my lunch, chewed my deadbeat ass out, and . . . for the small fee of $85 and court costs, entered a judgment against me for what I owed, interest, court cost, and attorney's fees.

In retrospect, I certainly should have known where the money was going. Mary had to have wicker furniture, you know, just the kind of sturdy stuff you need when you have three kids. Consequently, we replaced all of it about once a year. Our walls had wicker fans pinned all over them. We had enough silk plants to cover a mobster's funeral. Mary and the kids always had new clothes, and we threw out enough food every week to pull Somalia out of starvation, and that's not to mention keeping Mary happy with her collection of giant terracotta vases.

Naturally, when I got home from work that day, I was already in trouble for questioning her financial prowess and that fight lasted for the rest of that day and into the night. I'm still amazed that I would basically stand in one place as the shadows in the room moved, dutifully following the sun. The room would grow dusky and still Mary ranted on incessantly about how I was screwing her life up. A never-ending parade of ills that I had vested on her paraded across our living room like the circus from hell was in town. Elephants of indiscretion were hurried along by clowns of forced infidelity; Acrobats of heavy burden flipped and did summersaults over the heads of dagger throwers of broken hearts. At times, I was amazed at how good Mary's memory was.

I followed Mary to the bedroom as she simultaneously got ready for bed and wailed on about how big a mistake I was. She got into bed, covered herself with a quilt of self-righteousness, and moved on to my sexual problems starting with my gayness, and moving right on in to my wanting to bang every woman that got near the gravitational pull of my errant penis. The room began to brighten as the sun rolled up over the horizon and peeked into our bedroom window to see what chapter of Mary's miserable life we had fought up to in his absence.

I called into work for sick leave; the kids were made ready for school, and left as I relived all of the ills I had bestowed on Mary before she and I were even married. A few left hooks, and one or two right crosses were delivered and absorbed as names were called.

The kids got home from school, dinner was prepared as I was asked how I thought that made her feel that she had to hit me and call me names like that. Was I such a self-centered dick that I didn't care that this is what I had turned her life into? The kids went to bed as Mary pleaded with me to make her stop seeing her boyfriend. Shadows slid up the wall in dismal surrender to the dark. Street lights came on as my clothes were tossed around the house and out into the yard. I was told to get out or she would call the cops. I was told that if I left she would call work and tell them I was a wife beater. I followed Mary to the bedroom as she got ready for bed, taking time out to plead with me to stop being such an abusive asshole to her. I sat down on a bench in our bedroom . . .

. . . and passed out.

When I woke up, Mary was standing over me yelling at my heretofore unconscious body telling me that if I cared at all about her or our marriage I wouldn't be so callous as to go to sleep in the middle of us "working things out." Copious amounts of wine were consumed in between accusations being hurled and tears of desperation being shed. Non-present people were accused of unknown abuse, and incoherent speech gave way to mumbling, gave way to vomit, gave way to silence.

I picked Mary's limp body out of the filthy bed, changed the bed clothes, cleaned her up, put her back into bed, and fell asleep in a chair. Another day another dollar. Tomorrow back to the salt mines. Who gives a shit?

* * *

Awesome. My eye twitch is back and I didn't sleep at all last night. I keep a happy face on so that I don't have to pull my wife and friends into this cesspool with me.

FIFTEEN

One night we were coming back from dinner at a local pizza restaurant. I loved that place because the waitresses all hated me, the food was a buffet so the chances of them spitting or whatever in my food was slim, and they left me alone. As we got close to the entrance of the trailer park, I saw the back end of a car sticking out of a fairly deep ditch. I pulled off to the side of the road, told Mary and the kids to wait in the car and I ran across the two lane country road to see if anyone was hurt.

When I got to the driver's side of the car I froze. The driver was still in there, slumped over the steering wheel, apparently unconscious, and . . . it was a female. My dilemma was instantly and frightening clear to me. However, even though you may think you already know, let me back up and add some pertinent information. I've made it abundantly clear how jealous Mary was; however a few months prior to the incident I am retelling here, Mary had made an "out of the blue" request. Her mother had gotten cancer and died in Florida where she was living with her other daughter's boyfriend, (honestly I couldn't make this stuff up). Mary never wanted me to meet her mother because she was sure that the two of us would run

106

off together, I guess back to Florida, so they were still estranged when her mother passed.

As is the case with most people, her mother's mortality got Mary thinking. She did not think about her own mortality as most people might, or even about mine—As I said before, I was worth way more dead than alive—so instead it got Mary to start thinking about what would happen if I was the one that contracted some sort of heinous illness and was forced to be hospitalized. I mean, that could have horrific consequences for her. She imagined me being laid up in a hospital bed while she had to endure women coming in the room all hours of the day and night fawning over me and touching me and she knew that I, being the insensitive lump of shit that I was, would probably let them. She told me that she could never stand to watch that, and she made me promise that if anything ever happened to me like that I would never allow myself to be put in the hospital, and that I would never go to a doctor about it. After all doctors' offices were chock full of harlot nurses who only have a job like that in the first place so they can sink their hooks into someone like me.

I had absolutely no problem whatsoever making a promise

107

like that because I actually relished the thought of having a full blown heart attack and dying right on the spot. I actually had been day dreaming about just that sort of thing happening to me, the sooner the better.

What I hadn't considered was what my actions would be if it was someone else's life that hung in the balance. Was I going to be willing to make that sort of life or death decision so cavalierly when it was someone else's life? And for that matter, was Mary so disconnected from reality that she was going to demand that I allow someone to expire simply to satisfy her enormous insecurities?

I was about to find out.

Back to the scene of the crime.

When we last left our hero, I was standing at the driver's side of a car that was sticking face down in a muddy ditch on a dark country road. A woman is slumped over the steering wheel, not moving, and there isn't another car anywhere in sight. I've always heard that you never know what you're going to do in any given situation until the actual time comes. Then you won't have time to think about it. So when I saw it was a woman in the car I panicked and ran around to the passenger's side. Why? Who the hell knows?

Personally I think it because there wasn't an evil woman on that side of the car. In fact, as I could see from the driver's side, there was no one on that side . . . or anywhere else in the car. I walked up out of the ditch praying that I would see another car coming. The only things I saw in the road were three kids and a pissed off Mary.

"Well aren't you going to go back down there and help out your drunken little girl friend?" she asked, arms folded in definite body punctuation.

Just then another car pulled up, a man got out and hurried down the embankment.

"Go on," Mary said, "you're going to miss your chance. Just leave your wife and kids standing in the street all alone while you chase after another woman."

I walked back up to the car and said, "Let's go."

"Are you sure? Are you okay with another man taking care of your little woman over there? Oh yeah, I forgot of course you're okay with another man taking care of what you're not able to".

I pulled into the entrance of the park and went home. Mary was quiet until we got in the house. She went back to the bedroom to sulk and I followed behind her like a good little spineless whipping boy to take my lumps.

Sun up . . . sun down . . . bitch, bitch, bitch . . . sun up . . .
degrade, degrade, degrade . . .

Fuck it. Who cares? I have to die eventually, don't I?

SIXTEEN

Mary fancied herself a country western music writer/singer/superstar. So through some connection that I still haven't figured out (probably just as well) she found a band that was playing at a place called "The Kentucky Lounge." Whatever picture the name "Kentucky Lounge" conjures up in your mind is probably exactly what this place looked like. The building was so depressing on the outside that even the paint was trying to escape to some place more interesting. There was a giant, gravel parking lot in front that just screamed to be filled with hundreds of pickup trucks sporting gun racks and hayseeds in flannel shirts with a can of PBR permanently affixed to the palm of one hand. The inside made the outside look very inviting. Mary and I drove out to the bar one evening to listen to the band and talk to them about working with her. They were pretty good. The band leader seemed to be a typically genuine "howdy ma'am" nice guy, and they were excited about the possibility of getting some studio time with Mary.

One night I came home from a late shift and the house was lunatic free. The kids were all sleeping soundly but Mary was gone. So off I drive to do my duty as a concerned husband looking for my wife. It wasn't really that difficult because there really was only one place that she could possibly be. When I got to the parking lot of The Kentucky Lounge, I made a few passes around a slalom course of various four wheel drive pickup trucks each sporting a gun rack, a hayseed with a death grip on a PBR can, and a set of fake boobs that were actually life support systems for giant hairdos. I was looking for Mary's car, but it was no place to be seen. That left only one alternative.

I knew the hotel that Mary and her boyfriend stayed in because she told me all about it while she was telling me, with great angst, every sexual thing that he did to her that night. I knew why she was telling me in the first place: it was entirely my fault she was there, and hearing how many different ways she got nailed was my penance. When she regaled me with the blow by blow (pun totally intended) description I didn't understand her tragic demeanor at first. Then it came to me—she was the victim again, and I was her abuser. If I hadn't been such an insensitive turd, then she would not have had to be in a hotel getting her ass pounded out flat. The really sad part is that I finally got it, because I was starting to think like that as well.

After a short pass through the hotel parking lot, I saw her car.

"Great," I thought. "Now what? Go up to the room for a confrontation that I knew would be insane. Let the cops show up so I could get arrested and put the final nail in the coffin of my career?" To be perfectly honest, I would rather have been at home enjoying the peace and quiet until she was fully serviced and returned home. Anything else I was going to do was going to be because it was expected out of me.

I drove home and called the front desk of the hotel asking if anyone by her boyfriend's name had registered that night. (Of course I knew his name. That was nothing compared to the other things I knew about him). I got the room number and had the call transferred there. What surprised me was that Mary answered it. I told her that I had been out looking for her at the bar, and then the hotel.

Honestly, this many years later, I don't remember what exactly was said between us, all I remember thinking was that I thought it was very ironic that she finished the conversation by saying, "Look, I gotta go."

Naturally, we had to spend the entire next day talking about her Motel rendezvous, and I admit that I really had no problem talking about it, at least not a problem in the sense that Mary was screwing around on me. I accepted full responsibility for the fact that she had to go to someone else. After all, she told me it was going to happen if I didn't do anything to stop it, and obviously I hadn't. It never even occurred to me that this was a totally corrupt way of thinking. Year after year of sleep deprivation, head games that were happening so fast that there was no way in hell that I could keep up with them, and being completely shut off from any type of real outside influence had me completely broken, and I was ready to accept anything that Mary said.

One of the things that we talked about that day was that Mary decided not to use the band at the bar because they were "a bunch of assholes." Apparently, Mary and her boyfriend had actually stopped at the Kentucky Lounge before the hotel festivities began. They were sitting in the same seat at a booth near the dance floor. Mary had her back against the wall and had her legs laid across her boyfriend's lap while she played with his hair, kissed his neck and rubbed her hand on his crotch, and these miserable pricks in the band, that I had met and seemed to like me, had the audacity to give her "dirty looks" and never came over to talk to her.

The bastards!

Mary told me that the only way I was going to be able to keep her from continuing her sexual encounters was to talk to her about it every day. So, that's exactly what I did, like a dutiful little pawn, blissfully free of spine or free will. Every day I would initiate a conversation with my wife about what she was feeling about being forced to have sex with her gym partner . . . over and over again. She always acted like the perfect victim and I always made sure that I apologized for ever having put her in that position in the first place.

I guess the biggest mistake that I made was assuring her that I would never let anything like that happen again. The embarrassing part is that I actually took full responsibility for it simply because she told me it was my fault. Consequently, since she told me that it was up to me to keep her from doing it again, I accepted responsibility for that as well. I know now that there was no way that I was going to be able to keep her from going to him because that's what she wanted to do. Of course putting it on me like that was just insurance for her in the future, so she could place whatever she did at my feet.

A few weeks after this incident, Mary wanted the two of us

to go out like "regular people." I dreaded this because going out in public with Mary never ended well for me, and I guess "regular people" liked to return to the scene of the crime because we were going to the good ol' Kentucky Lounge. Thank God when we got there the house band was other than the one that I had met. After this many years, the exact events of the night in the bar are hazy. Kind of like a tour in Vietnam. I remember that Mary was totally hammered. At some point she made a big deal about the guy standing at the bar grabbing her ass as she walked by. She wanted me to go kick his ass. I wasn't about to because I still had semblance of mind enough to know that the incident probably never happened in the first place. We got in an argument, Mary got drunker, and said that if I wasn't going to do anything to stop it she might as well take him out to the parking lot and fuck him.

It was time to go.

Once we got in the car, there was a group of people standing around just outside the door of the bar talking. As we drove past them, Mary rolled her window down, hung half way out of it and screamed, "I love you, baby. If you want me, come and get me". I hauled her back in the car by the belt and she rewarded me good with a hot shot in the temple.

That car ride home was one of the strangest things that ever happened to me in a life filled with strange things. Mary reclined the seat back as far as it would go and started to read over the endless list of the ways that I had thus far fucked her life up. That certainly wasn't surprising, because I knew that was going to happen before we ever even left home. It started getting strange when she launched into a diatribe of reasons why she was in love with her boyfriend. Drunkenly, she rambled on and on about all the things that I was doing to thwart that budding romance. This morphed into her begging me to let her go to him. I would have gladly dropped her off at his house if I only knew where it was. Clearly, this was the only way that I was going to be able to get any peace and quiet that night. Hell, if I was lucky he might even keep her.

The begging gave way to pleading, and this gave way to an odd conversation between her and him, with him in absentia. I don't know if it was a reenactment of an actual conversation they had actually had, or if it was a conversation that she had wanted to happen in her head, or if she was completely cognizant of what she was doing and just messing with my head.

117

Whatever it was, eventually she began to systematically work her way out of her clothes. This was a new one. Piece by piece, each garment was shed and tossed carelessly into the backseat of the car. Eventually, Mary sat in the right seat of the car completely naked telling her invisible lover how much she wanted him and exactly what she wanted him to do to her.

That was when she started to masturbate as she gave a play by play of everything "he" was doing to her. While this was going, on all I could think about has how I was going to get her into the house without the neighborhood seeing it, and with any luck the kids wouldn't wake up. Once "they" got to the post coitus afterglow, she lay there in her "all together," wet with sweat and resumed begging me to let her go to him.

That was when she puked in the car.

Once we got home, I tried to park on the darkest part of the street I could find. I went into the house and grabbed a bathrobe, went back out to the car, wrapped Mary up in it, carried her into the house, and

put her to bed.

SEVENTEEN

Mary decided she wanted to live someplace warmer so I put in a request for a transfer to a couple of warmer places, and one of them was approved. I thought this was going to be just the thing we needed to start to get our life back on track. However, this would be my first hard life lesson that a change of scene will never fix a person's problems because they're going to take themselves along. You've got to fix yourself before anything else is going to help the situation.

I knew that Mary was still sneaking off to have a little sexual healing every chance she got, even though she told me she wasn't. But I figured that if I just separated the penis from the spouse, everything would be fine. I never considered that there would be penis floating around where we were going, just looking for an open vagina to fall into.

Being in the financial crapper as we were and due to the fact that this was a lateral move, the government wasn't going to pay for it. We got a U-haul with a tow dolly for my work beater. Mary would drive her Firebird that she leased and I would drive the truck, towing my car.

Naturally, we had no friends in the trailer court and I certainly didn't want anyone that I knew helping me for fear that they might mention the fact that there were actually women working in the same place I was. So, I was left to load the contents of a three bedroom, doublewide trailer, complete with the belongings of three teenage kids, and all of the crap from a tool shed into the biggest U-haul truck they had all by my lonesome.

To be fair, the oldest step son was fifteen, and he was an invaluable help, but there was only so much he could do.

The truck was jam packed to bulging, and my car was up on the tow dolly and hitched up to the truck the day before we were going to start south. We all crammed into the firebird and went to a local fast food place for a final trailer park calorie laden dinner, and then we returned to the empty trailer and moved off to our respective rooms for a fun night sleeping on the floor in sleeping bags. In the morning, our 1500 mile adventure would begin.

Well, we were supposed to begin our new life, but life with Mary was just one fun-filled surprise after another.

The sun came up, shedding light on spot where Mary's car usually sat. I only had one emotion: I was pissed because her final

120

vaginal probing was going to make us late getting on the road. The kids all wanted to know where Mommy was, and I worked hard to make half assed excuses for her as I paced back and forth in the parking lot next to the rental truck. I've looked back on that scene a lot since then, and in my rewritten historical reverie, I answer their questions by getting in the truck and heading out the driveway, leaving Mary to clean up her own mess.

Instead I paced back and forth in the street, and checked my watch.

A short time later, the black Firebird rolled up to the house. Mary was completely drained and had obviously won the gold medal in the all-out, no-holds-barred sex marathon from the night before. The kids questions about where she had been all night were answered with an offhand "I had some things I needed to do," and we all went into our empty home.

"Are you ready to go?" I asked. I didn't know if this was going to start a fight or not and at that point I didn't really care about that, or what she had been doing all night.

"I'm not going to be able to drive today," she said blankly. "I haven't gotten any sleep, and I know that I couldn't stay awake."

The only answer was the oldest boy. Having only his temporary driver's license meant that he was going to have to drive the Firebird with his mother, and I would drive the truck.

"I don't want him to drive my car," she whined. "He's going to screw it up somehow. Besides I need you to talk to me about this. That always helps me sleep."

I looked at her while I let this soak in and weighed my options. I was going to drive her car, while she relived her night of banging her boyfriend in a hotel. Her fifteen-year-old son with a temporary driver's permit, and all of the sense of responsibility of a two year old was going to drive the biggest rental truck they made, filled with all of our worldly possessions . . . including the other two kids (because they certainly couldn't listen to how their mom blew a stranger the night before), AND tow our other car. Or, I could argue with Mary, which would blow up into a full blown, knockdown drag out lasting who the hell knew how long while the days we had on our rental truck ticked down. And, to top off this little Vaudeville act, we still had no idea where we were going to live when we got to our new location . . .

A place, incidentally which no one in this moronic

melodrama had ever even visited before . . .

"Fine, let's go," I said. "What was the worst that could happen?"

I gave the brand new truck driver the once over in the cab, asked if he had any questions, fully understanding that he didn't even know enough to ask anything, and off we went. Job one before we ever even got on the interstate was to stop and get gas—hence the first dilemma. Luckily, he had the presence of mind to stop just inside the driveway to the gas station. He waited while I hooked up the car and start fueling, (Mary sat in the car and pouted), then I went back to the truck, maneuvered it to a gas pump, and filled it up.

Once on the road, Mary started telling me everything that happened the night before. Thankfully, I was numb to this bullshit so I could concentrate on driving with one eye looking forward, and the other watching in the rear view mirror, waiting to see either a giant rental truck go careening out of control, killing the driver and two passengers. Or, watch the same giant truck getting pulled over by the police so I could explain why I ever let a fifteen year old drive it by himself. I have to say that he did a great job considering his limited experience.

Someplace many hours into this trip from hell, I noticed that the headlights on the rental truck began flashing on and off. I thought, "Well, we were lucky we got this far before the problems started." I pulled over into the breakdown lane of the interstate and the truck pulled up close behind me. Traffic whipped past us and I was just starting to get out of the car to tell everybody to stay in the truck so they wouldn't get hit when I saw my stepson's smiling face in the side window. "How'd he get up here that fast?" I thought.

"What's up?" I asked.

"Nothing," he said, still smiling "I just wanted to come up and talk for a while."

"Listen," I began. Then I looked in the rearview mirror to make sure that the other two weren't getting out "just to talk" as well. That was when I noticed that the truck was getting smaller. The other two kids had already gotten out and were standing off to the right side of the car. When my step son had gotten out of the truck, he had left it in neutral and didn't set the break. The fact that we were sitting on a fairly steep uphill grade didn't help.

Slowly gravity was dragging everything we owned back down a hill as the car on the tow dolly started to gently arch off to the right, which would put it over the side of about 100 feet of drop off. I jumped out of the car and ran for the cab of the truck. My step son ran behind me and when I got to the left door of the cab, he kept going. I grabbed the door handle and was trying to jump up on the running board. The truck was moving fast enough now to force me to jog to keep up with it and time my jump. I knew that I was only going to have one chance. As I leapt up onto the running board, I watched with distracted horror as my stepson ran between the backing truck and the tow dolly.

I jumped up in the cab and slammed the breaks on just about the same time I saw his worried face appear in the right window. I sat there shaking for a while trying to collect myself as he apologized up one side and the other. I told him that it sure as hell wasn't his fault because he had no damned business driving that truck in the first place. Then I apologized to him for ever putting him in that situation in the first place.

I went back to the car and Mary asked if everything was alright. Again, I never thought about this until right this minute, but she never even got out of the car. Someone else could take care of what she caused in the first place and she could just sit there as a spectator. I told her that I really needed to drive the truck and asked her if she felt up to driving yet. Naturally she whined that she was too tired even after sleeping most of the way to where we currently were.

"I don't want another situation like this to happen," I told her.

"Then take care of it. Explain to him what he did wrong and make sure that it doesn't happen again," she said.

Case closed.

When I think about it, Mary would have made a great bureaucrat. Her tact in problem solving was exactly like the federal governments'; fix whatever the last problem was so that it can't happen again, then act surprised when something else goes wrong. They seem allergic to problem solving by using forward thinking.

I don't remember now if we stopped someplace on the way to our new hometown, but I'm sure that we had to. It was one hell of a long trip and there was no way that a fifteen-year-old driver was going to be able to keep it up for twelve or fifteen hours straight. I do remember that when we pulled into the big city, I was driving the truck, and we hadn't even made reservations at a hotel. We just drove through town and stopped at the first high rise Holiday Inn that we came to.

I had the truck for another 4 or 5 days and I was going to be on leave from work for another week. We parked the truck. The entire brood crammed into the Firebird and off we went, as clueless as a newborn baby, looking for a place to live. I knew that this was a half assed way to do things from soup to nuts. But I also knew that this was the only option that Mary would allow. I couldn't have called apartments in the area to try and set up living arrangements before we got there because the chances that it would be a woman I had to deal with were pretty much a given, and Mary would have gone bat-shit if I actually worked things out with a woman no matter what the reason was. I also knew that Mary certainly wasn't going to take any form of initiative because that was my job and the fact that she was making it impossible for me to do it was my problem.

One or two days into this fiasco, we found what was referred to in this area as "patio homes" for rent. These are basically single floor townhouses that are all connected together and they have a postage-sized patio in back, so you could sit outside in fenced-in confinement and look at the sky. I honestly didn't care if it was a

$2000 a month refrigerator box under an overpass by this time. I had been dodging, or being hateful to waitresses, maids, and gas station clerks for days now, and it was starting to take its toll on me. I needed to get into someplace that I could hide from the world, go to work, come home, and fend off Mary's craziness.

EIGHTEEN

The career that I was in required me to pass a second class airman's physical once a year and this physical had to be done by certified flight surgeons, and it had to be conducted during my normal working hours. This caused Mary real heartburn right from the beginning because someone was going to be touching me and see me naked. The fact that this was usually a 200 year old man was irrelevant to her.

When we were first married, physical day was pretty easy to get around. We were scheduled at the doctor's office first thing in the morning, so we weren't expected to go into work first. We'd just go to the doctor's office then when our physical was done we'd go to work. Since Mary had to accompany me to ALL things, including physicals, I would just take her with me. I'd be as shitty as I could to the receptionist, try to keep my blood pressure down by working Jedi mind tricks on myself, drop her off back at home, then drive like hell to get to work.

Now things were made almost impossible by the FAA. They wanted to put a stop to waste, so we all had to show up for work, then leave for our physical, then get back to work. Naturally, Mary thought I was lying about that and accused me of taking time off work so I could go out and get laid. I used to think that if I had been doing a quarter of as much screwing as she thought I was, I would only weigh ninety lbs and have a permanent hole worn in the side of my penis. So once a year, I would drive thirty minutes into work, work there for an hour or so, then I would drive like a maniac back home, pick up Mary, go to the doctor's office, shit on any women that I might encounter, take my physical, placate Mary, and calm any angst that she may have about the operation, then drive like hell to get back to work so that I wasn't gone too long, and get my ass chewed for not being back on time.

The best part was sitting in the waiting room, scared to death that someone I worked with was going to come in and make some offhanded comment about a woman at work. Not about any impropriety or anything, just simply mention that women *actually worked* in the same place that I did. If that were to happen, I knew that it would be used as fight fodder for the rest of my life.

Eventually, I told Mary that since terrorists had hijacked TWA847, she would no longer be able to go to the doctor's office with me since the office was actually at another secure government facility. In fact, I told her that she and the kids would never be able to come to where I worked again. This was easy to pass off because security at work had always been high. A fence surrounded the parking lot and you needed the code to get the gate opened. Once there, you needed a cipher code to get in the door and another one to get into the actual operating quarters.

I worked very hard to keep my job separated from the lunacy that was my marriage. If nothing else, it was embarrassing, but due to conduct and discipline, mixing the two could be life changing. One night during a particularly horrible fight, Mary had threatened to call the police and tell them that I had hit her. She wanted desperately for me to spend the night in jail. I thought it was because she was all cranked up at me, but later on I realized that the only way she could get all the attention that she so desperately needed was to have me be arrested for domestic violence. I told her that if she called the cops, she would look like an idiot because I had never even pretended to hit her. She told me that she would tell the police that I had hit her in the stomach so it wouldn't show.

"Who do you think they're going to believe?" she asked

This was the mid 1980's and the sad fact was, she was right.

If nothing else, the police would have told me to spend the night someplace else and the next time they came to my house they would remember that they had already been out there once for domestic violence. The police threat continued on for quite a long time.

One night during a fight, she had locked herself in the bedroom so she could get drunk and I heard her talking to someone on the phone, asking them what they would do if they ever found out that one of their employees was beating his wife. I went into the kitchen and picked up the extension and the voice I heard on the other end explaining that this would be cause for termination was one of the supervisors I worked for.

I couldn't believe it. Why on earth would she ever put HER income in jeopardy? She sure as hell wasn't working and never had. If I got fired that would be it. A few days later I got the answer to my question. We were having another of our endless family discussions where everybody got to get together to talk about what an asshole I was. I had asked the boys to cut the grass and they ignored me and left for the park. When I got home from work and found nothing had been done, I grounded them for a week. So during our "family meeting", Mary told me to ask them if grounding did anything for them. To me, this was like asking a convicted killer if incarceration would do anything to change him. Of course they said no.

While I was trying to bring this conversation back to some kind of semblance of order, Mary told the youngest boy to tell me why he thought I would get so pissed off when I told them to cut the grass and they didn't. He told me that it was because I knew that they did a better job than I did and I hated that. I was reeling from the sheer lack of logic here, but then he was thirteen years old at the time. Then I noticed that Mary was looking at me like, "even they know you're a dick."

That was when she told him to tell me what he thought about my job. I was trying to figure out what opinion any thirteen year old could possibly have about an adult's job, when he said that I let it come before my family and I should quit and find something else to do.

I looked at Mary, and she was sitting there with that sanctimonious "see" look on her face.

"Obviously you think that too," I said to her.

"How could you possibly not think that?" she asked like she was addressing a frog turd.

I knew that a lot of my friends allowed this job to wipe out their families, but that was due to drug and alcohol abuse, or after work whoring around. I wasn't doing any of those things. If I wasn't at work, I was home working my ass off in the yard or on the house or trying to calm Mary down.

"Tell him what you think he should do," she said to the thirteen-year-old accuser.

"I think that he should quit and get a job in construction," was his serious reply.

I thought, *"Ain't that cute. This kids think that I should just shit can my job because I told him to cut the grass. I'm making more money than two thirds of my high school graduating class. I have no other skills. This is all I've done since I was eighteen, and I have zero college."*

"And you?" I said to Mary.

"I've thought that for a long time," she said to me "There are plenty of construction jobs out there, and you could stop being so wrapped up in what you do."

I realize now that this was a conversation that they all had had several times before while I was gone. Apparently, they had it every time I had expected something to get done around the house and they decided to do something else. I knew that to someone like Mary who was living at the top of the insecurity ladder, and never graduated from high school in the first place, and had only been associated with self-employed construction workers that were barely getting by, my job was intimidating. I also knew that working behind a wall of security tore all control that Mary had on me right out of her hands for at least forty hours a week. She wanted to put a stop to that.

That's one thing that *wasn't* going to happen. The family conversation ended the same way that they usually did. I was a piece of shit, and I expected too much out of everybody. During one of these conversations, the oldest kid said that all he wanted out of life was some kind of a job . . . he didn't care doing what. He wanted to live in a rented mobile home and drive a used Camaro. After a few short minutes of reflection, he said that he'd change that to a used motorcycle because the Camaro was too much responsibility. His mother asked him what his biggest dream would be and he said he wanted to save up $5000 dollars and buy a rollercoaster.

He was seventeen at the time.

I never asked anyone to do anything after that. They all just did whatever they wanted, and it would show later in life as the first two dropped out of high school, and the last one went from As and Bs to Cs and Ds in his last two years.

At least they didn't have to cut the grass anymore.

NINETEEN

While we were still in our crappy little "patio home," Mary found a restaurant-bar that was close to us she wanted to go to. We went, and it became someplace that we actually spent a lot of time in. At first there were no female bar tenders—we spent all of our time at the bar, and not in the restaurant—and all of the usual suspects that hung out there were men. It is a psychological fact that people use a significant emotional experience to mark a point in their life. For example, among a group of people someone might say, "Was that before or after Dad died?" and everyone would know what they were talking about. Or someone might say about a date, " . . . no, that had to be 1991 because it was before the hurricane." My significant emotional experience was finding that bar.

For quite a while between moving away from the Kentucky Lounge and finding "our" bar at our new home, Marry had been having phone conversations with the boyfriend she had left behind. All of these occurred while I was at work, and although Mary had told me all about them, I didn't have to actually listen to it so I really didn't care. That ship had sailed a long time ago.

Then one night, the phone rang at about one o'clock in the

morning, and it was him. She laid in our bed talking to her fuck buddy for an hour or two while I sat in the living room. When she was done, she came out and asked me if I was alright. I should have just said I was fine and went to bed. Instead I said, "How the hell am I supposed to feel? You just got done shooting the shit with your boyfriend in our bed."

All these years later, I remember that this spawned a giant fight, no violence, but all my clothes were tossed out in the front yard. I made a mental note that saying anything but "have a good time" when it came to Mary's infidelity just wasn't worth the time. After a few weeks of these phone calls, Mary came to me and said that her boyfriend wanted to meet her in Atlanta so they could get some things straightened out. I knew that I had two choices. One say it was fine, she goes to Atlanta and gets drilled to a fare-thee-well, then comes home and I'm only out airfare. Or I could say what I was thinking, get the shit beaten out of me for it, and stay up for two or three days going over the list of every real or imagined fault and wrong I've committed.

Mary was off to Atlanta, and I was left to explain to the kids why she wasn't really going to see her boyfriend.

For the three days she was there getting laid, while I was taking care of the kids, and the house, and working. Mary called a few times a day to tell me how things were going. She told me how many times they had sex, alternated between complaining about how it didn't live up to her expectations, and describing things to me that would make a porno star blush. Prior to that, I only *thought* I didn't care anymore, but after that I had gone into full shutdown mode. Every day was just another in a string of unbearable humiliating days that followed me around like an insane clown parade from hell. Mary could do anything she wanted and my own death couldn't come soon enough. Sometimes, I would find myself driving to work and daydreaming about having a heart attack and dying right there. People always said that stress caused heat disease, but it hadn't taken me yet, and I was getting impatient.

After the Atlanta episode, Mary and I were sitting in *our* bar one evening and she was telling me that she was interested in one of the regulars who was in there every single time we were. So, I told her that I thought she should pursue it. I didn't have any problem with that. I didn't realize it at the time, but I had sunk to a new low in my life I was actually actively involved in picking out sexual prospects for Mary. After I extricated myself from that mess, I told myself the reason I would acquiesce to helping Mary find guys to bang, with the same kind of support that I would give her when it came to her "music" career, was because I just didn't care about her anymore, which was definitely true. But if I am going to be totally introspective here and try to explain things for the way that they actually were, I would have to say that by this time in my life, anything that resembled the old me was long gone. I think that anything Mary might have wanted me to do I would have gone along with if I thought it would make her happy and cut down on the violence and crazy in my life.

Look at the followers of Jim Jones. These were seemingly normal people that had been transfigured into people that were not only *able* to drink the poison Kool-Aid but who also administered it to their own children. Or look at the purple track suit, identical tennis shoe wearing cult that all committed suicide. You see the same type of behavior that I was exhibiting. The only thing that I cared about was making sure that Mary got the things in her life that she wanted. Not because I loved her, but because all sense of reason had been beaten, screamed or threatened out of me a long time ago. I think about the pictures of Patty Hearst standing in the bank with an automatic weapon. If someone had simply walked up to her when she was her former self, handed her an assault rifle and told her to rob a bank, she would have certainly told them to fuck off.

Instead, not only was she there willingly helping her captors, she thought she was doing it of her own free will. I also thought I was doing this of my own free will. Years later after I ran away and hid from Mary, I reestablished contact with my family. I was sitting on my parents' back porch and we were talking about the events of the past eleven years in my absence. I told my mother the same story that I'm retelling here, and she was horrified. The look that she had on her face clearly said there was something seriously wrong with me, and that look would keep me from ever telling that story again to anyone other than my current wife.

Until I began writing it right this minute.

I realize that my very first instinct was to legitimize my actions by making it look like I was feeling something other than what was actually going on in my own head at the time. In fact, I really no longer cared about Mary, or myself for that matter, but that wasn't the reason why things went down the dark path that they did.

My entire reason for existence at this point was to support Mary in whatever way she wanted. If that way was to make sure that she could bang as many people as she could, then I was going to, very dispassionately, make sure that that happened.

I feel as though I'm doing a piss poor job of getting anyone to understand this. What I do know is that there are people, men and women alike, who will read this and think "that's exactly what I did. I can't explain it either but at least I know it wasn't just because I was flawed or weak." Only for those readers do I go on. The rest of you can sit in any type of judgment you like. Just remember that no one ever really knows how they are going to react in any given situation until they are actually there.

So, all of this being said, I came home from work one night at 11:30 to find that Mary was gone. The kids weren't sure where she was and she hadn't said when she would be home. This wasn't new; she had done it plenty of times before. The first few times it happened I just waited at home until she got back. This was met with an amazing amount of wrath, screaming and crying, because if I cared about her at all, I would have gone looking for her. She could have been kidnapped, or killed in a car accident, or been in the hospital someplace, and I would just be sitting there in the dark waiting to find out what happened.

The fact that in every single incident she had been out either getting laid in a car or a shitty motel room was irrelevant. So after I was set straight, I dutifully went looking for her. My next mistake was that I had gone looking for her alone. Mary said that the only reason I would do that was so I could get out of the house and try to pick up women. During this insane argument I pointed out the duality of her position. I was going out to try to find her while she was having an affair and she was pissed at me because I might try and pick someone up. Amidst the landing of a few good punches, and a hail storm of insults, I was told that only an insensitive piece of shit like me would throw the fact that she was FORCED to go outside the marriage to get what she needed in her face. Any decent man would accept the world that they had made for their wife and try to fix it. She also pointed out that not even my own parents wanted to have anything to do with me. That was just how big of a load of shit I was. I couldn't argue with her there. I hadn't talked to my family for years at that time . . . all in Mary's name.

After she laid down the ground rules for looking for her, I

had to take one of the kids with me on the great Mary hunt. As I write this, I realize how asinine this sounds. Mary is out getting laid so I *have* to go looking for her, and I *have* to take one of her kids with me so they can make sure that I'm not doing anything tawdry. This well-thought-out operational plan from hell was about to blow up in our faces.

I took the youngest with me. Why him? After all these years, I can't remember. We loaded up in my barely drivable POS and off we went in search of his mother. The first place I thought to look was in the parking lot of the bar we had been frequenting. Sure enough, there sat Mary's black Firebird and through the fogged up windows I could see two people sitting in it. I panicked, I knew exactly what was going on and I was trying to drive past it as quickly as I could to avoid her son seeing what was going on. The only saving grace I had was the fact that the windows were foggy, and for the time being both heads were above the dashboard.

"Hey," he said, pointing at his mother's car, "that's Mom's car right there."

"Nope," I said looking straight ahead "I don't think it is."

"Sure it is, all the chrome is blacked out, just like hers."

"No, I think your wrong on this one. Let's keep looking. I think I see her over there," I said pointing to the other side of the parking lot.

Just then as I was passing her car, I saw Mary's head disappear below the dashboard. We were past the car now and it was time to go home.

"Oops," I said. "I guess I was wrong. That's not her after all. Let's keep looking."

So we went home. He went off to bed, and I sat in the dark waiting for Mary to get home. Naturally when she got there, she had the same demeanor that she always did after a sexual go around. It's hard to describe, but she acted like a coal miner that had just come back from a tough day at work when they realize that this is the job they'll be doing for the rest of their lives and there's no way out. She was always despondent and always regaled me with every last detail of what she and her latest trophy had done. Of course she had blown him, but she said she did that because she didn't want to. Actually I believe that, I think she really loved to be forced to do things that she didn't want to do. Then he banged her right there in the parking lot of the bar, and that was a problem because he wasn't that good at it.

I actually apologized to her for that . . . and she accepted it.

She and her new boyfriend spent a lot of time together after that, whenever I worked a dayshift and the kids were at school or I was working a nightshift and she could make some excuse to them, she would be off spending time with him. They went to the park and had sex, and went to the beach and had sex, and sat in the car and had sex. I guess he really knew how to show a girl a good time. The problem that was beginning to manifest itself for Mary, and one that she never saw coming, was that this guy was starting to get attached to her and was thinking about taking her away from me. Mary was never going to let this happen. I was able to keep her ass deep in terra cotta vases, new clothes, and cheap jewelry from QVC. He was a hair dresser working in someone else's shop and couldn't even afford to take her out for dinner.

One afternoon, he called her for a last minute rendezvous. Unfortunately for him, Mary and I were going through the early stages of a several day fight and I had taken sick leave to show her that I was committed to fix the unfixable. So, when he called, I answered the phone. Apparently he never heard the old adage, "if a man answers hang up," and he had started to feel his oats with his married girlfriend. He started bitching me out for treating Mary like shit all the time. I had no idea what she had been telling him, but I'm fairly sure that in between trying new sexual positions in the car, she was whining to him about how shitty I had made her life. After all, that was exactly what she was doing with me when I was in his position several years before.

I was already cranked up from many hours trying to talk reason to a lunatic, so he and I got into a major yelling match on the phone. That changed to testosterone-laden threats, which changed to direct challenges, I found out he was actually calling from the bar, and off Mary and I went to confront her newest boyfriend.

We no sooner got out of the car in the parking lot and he came running out of the door of the bar. I'm not sure what I looked like, but I was relishing this with every fiber of my body. I had a lot of years of eating shit stored up inside of me and I was about to unleash it on this poor, dumb, unsuspecting asshole that was fast walking his way into a long hospital stay. Whatever the look was that I had on my face, it stopped him in his tracks well out of striking range. I don't remember now all of the stupid shit that was screamed back and forth between us in the parking lot that day, but I do know that as Mary stood there watching it, she saw something that she didn't like—probably the fact that this guy was getting attached to her. She made plans right there to put a stop to it.

The confrontation ended with both of us going our separate ways, and as is typical, both of us claiming victory. Mary and this guy had one last go around when he took her to some other bar one night. As the story goes, some guy was hitting on her pretty hard at the bar, and Mary was going with it. Her date, like the rest of the men in Mary's life, was too stupid to do the math and realize that he had just become me and this other clown was now him. So, as she tells the story, her date takes her out in the parking lot, rips her clothes off, apparently to her initial protest, and bangs the shit out of her right in the parking lot as the bar was closing and people were walking all around the car.

Mary thought that was pretty cool and it showed her how much he cared for her.

Shortly after that, Mary broke things off with this guy. I knew that was coming after she told me that last story. Too bad he didn't. After it was over, Mary and I were back in that bar again and he was sitting a few chairs down, drunk as hell.

"You know," he was slurring to his drunken buddies, "she's a pretty good fuck, but she can't give head worth a shit."

I slammed my hands down on the bar. "That's it, asshole, "I said to him. "Let's go."

We were both up off our bar stools and I followed him out the door. Once outside on the sidewalk, he stopped instantly and spun around, telegraphing a huge, wide, right hook that I was too stupid to duck out of the way of and he connected with my left cheek. I was surprised that he didn't hit any harder than Mary did and I started laughing uncontrollably.

"I think you missed fuck nuts," I said, laughing. That really pissed him off and that was when the rest of the barflies showed up and separated us. That was the last I ever saw of him, and as far as I know, that was the end of he and Mary.

It most certainly wasn't the end of the penis patrol in that same bar.

TWENTY

As I had said before, Mary had her own interesting ideas about handling money and the mysterious world of high finance. In the beginning of our relationship, well before Mary had transformed me into the sniveling little yes man that I had become, I would ask her where the hell all the money was going. I had a pretty good income, and we were living from paycheck to paycheck. I mean exactly that too—just as we were running on our last dollar, the next check would come, and that's all we had. No savings, no IRA, nothing. Her answer was always the same: it took a lot of money to feed and clothe three kids and according to Mary, if I hadn't spent all of my life up to that point being a selfish prick that only lived for himself, I would know that. Well, what I did know was there were a lot of people I worked with, making the same thing I was, with three and sometimes more kids, and they were getting along just fine and actually putting money aside.

Mary had an interesting view of a relatively new service that the banks were just coming out with at that time. The ATM card. If she went to the ATM to withdraw money, and the machine gave it to her, then that meant that we must have had the money available in the account to begin with. Forget about the fact that there might have been checks still out, or bank fees, or whatever. If the bank gave her the money through the ATM, then the money was there. After all, weren't bank people getting paid to keep track of your money in the first place, and if they didn't know how much you had in your account, then who did?

Naturally, there were a ton of overdrafts and returned check fees from the bank as well as from the businesses that had been stiffed. Naturally, the bank simply deducted these charges directly from the checking account. Of course they weren't sneaky about it or anything. They clearly noted the deductions on the bank statement when it came to us. Unfortunately, Mary had a bad habit of tossing the bank statements in the trash when they came in . . . usually unopened. She never balanced the check book, and she kept track of all the checks she wrote in her head.

So when we got a refund from the IRS at tax time, she deposited it in our checking account and started writing checks on it. Of course, at the same time she was writing checks the bank was taking nearly all of it back as payment for penalties that had yet to be paid. Mary went ape shit because the bank was *stealing* from us. I can't even count the number of times we owed people money, including her own father, and she simply refused to pay them. Now the bank had her by the proverbial balls. She didn't have to worry about paying her debt. This time the bank simply took it back.

Naturally, we took all of our money out of that bank because they weren't to be trusted and went someplace else. Instantly it was the exact same scenario as before. Overdraw the checking account through the ATM just because it gave you the money, disregard any ATM fees, and then disregard any overdraft fees. At the same time, we were getting notices for unpaid bills, ignored late fees, and unpaid car payments. I didn't know any of this because I never saw the mail, and Mary sure as hell wasn't going to say anything to me because of the fit I threw before.

All of this came to a head when we went to a boat rental place for some special occasion or another and the rental company confiscated my card. The attendant cut it into little pieces right in front of me. Mary was pissed because they had no right to do that. I, on the other hand, knew that in certain cases they had *every* right to if they had been instructed to by the company when they tried to make a charge on it. On the way home, I asked how the hell that

152

could have happened, and that was when I was given my crash course in Creative Financing 102. Mary would pick the bills to pay and the ones to shit can. We were already making the minimum payment on all three credit cards that we had so we couldn't cut down on our cash outflow there, so some got paid and some got put off. The ones that got put off got paid the next time and the ones that got paid before got put off. AND . . . here's the great one . . . the ones that were coming from a company that had sent her a shitty note telling her to pay her bills didn't get anything. She'd show them, by God.

Mary was about to learn that it really did mean something when a company paid the $85 court fee and sued you

She was always looking for an angle to get around whatever her responsibilities might be. So when the second bank started taking our money, Mary decided that no banks were to be trusted and we were going to take all of our money out of them and handle everything with cash or money orders. By this time, I was far from even putting up the most modest of arguments against this—or anything else, for that matter.

I started to say that Mary and I fought nearly every day by

then, but that wouldn't have been accurate. Nearly every day, Mary found something that I did or said that proved I didn't really love her. If it wasn't that, it was something that I didn't do, or didn't say. Hour after hour after miserable hour I would switch back and forth between trying to put up a half-assed defense without giving her more to be pissed about, and totally agreeing with her to try and keep things from getting out of hand and physical . Consequently, being totally down the financial toilet was the least of my worries.

At any rate, at first we kept a checking account at a local bank so I could cash my checks, but that too would turn sour. Mary wasn't keeping up with checking account fees, and for that matter, neither was I, but remember, all of the family financial matters had been taken out of my hands because I was incompetent. So eventually, the checking account not only dwindled down to nothing, after a while, it was actually in the red.

Now, since Mary was completely incapable of accepting responsibility for anything she did, we were forced to take my pay check to the check cashing store. At the time, I was making about $1200 a check and they took 10% of that right off the top. Then we would by money orders for every bill we had. Utilities, credit cards, everything.

We were sliding down a money pit so fast and so deep that we were never going to see the surface again, and to make things even better, Mary used the time I was gone at work to catch up on her sleep, clean the house and watch QVC for great deals on crap that we didn't need and sure as hell couldn't afford. She would wait for me to come home or have a day off so we could load up in the car and do everything from grocery shopping to money order buying. Every time I tried to get the kids to help do anything around the house, we'd have another family meeting, chaired by Mary to discuss what a demanding prick I was. It was easier to just handle it myself, but I was a mess.

TWENTY-ONE

Just prior to the money order fiasco, Mary decided we needed to buy a house. To be honest with you, I knew that that was exactly what we should have done. I certainly made enough money to afford one and we were raising three kids, plus the rent was just going down the toilet with nothing to show for it. On the other hand, the thought of owning a home scared the hell out of me. I mean, we were just barely able to keep up with owning a car, and our money picture looked like Nightmare on Elm Street.

So Mary found a house about thirty minutes from work that accepted VA financing so we could work with no money down. The place was actually a very nice, brand new, three bedroom, two bathroom, ranch type house, in an equally new housing development. So we got another rental truck and off we went to a new home and an overabundance of conversation about a new life.

That was about the time that Mary's Firebird was repossessed.

One of the bill paying MO's that she used was that if any of the creditors gave her any shit at all about having missed a payment, she would simply quit paying them. In her words, "they were being jerks," and she wasn't going to put up with that out of anybody. Apparently, the fact that we had borrowed money, goods, or services from them in good faith, promising faithfully that we would, in fact, pay them back . . . albeit with a money order . . . didn't mean anything to her, and I guess she thought she held far more clout than she actually did.

This set off a series of emotional carnival rides.

I found out later that she had actually been sent several late notices, followed by a poorly written chain of letters promising repossession, followed by more than a few phone calls. According to Mary, she figured that the car had been purchased 1500 miles away. They would never be able to find it when they came after it, and even if they used our last known address it would have been at the patio home. Hell, that was at least five miles away from where we lived now.

So I wake up one morning, walk outside, and there's an empty driveway. I called the police to report the theft, and I was told that there had been a repossession at our address the night before. I was destroyed because I had always been financially responsible.

157

Mary was pissed and wanted blood. I called the bank, and they referred me to the collection agent. In my mind, I only had one option: to kiss however much ass I needed to in order to try and get our car back. I was on the phone with that guy for over an hour pleading with him, and offering to do whatever it took to rectify this. Clearly it was too late, the car was gone, and I had a repossession to add to my growing financial repertoire.

When I got off the phone, Mary had a lovely Jackson Pollack plastered all over her face and I knew I was screwed. Apparently, in retrospect, I didn't think that I was screwed enough.

"I thought you were making the payments?" I asked the quaking Mary.

"So let me see if I get this right," she said slowly as her mouth turned a very interesting shade of teal and eggplant. "These assholes come to your house in the middle of the night, they steal your car without so much as a notice, then you spend an hour blowing this same jerk off on the phone, and your answer to all of this is to accuse me!"

"Well, they don't just come and steal your car out of your driveway . . . with the police having full knowledge I'm pretty sure that they're in the right."

"Unbelievable! You just got your car stolen and instead of taking care of your wife, you support the thief and not me."

She gestured with her hand and made a face like she just found a giant rat trying on her best panties. "Look at you. You're disgusting. Just what kind of a man are you anyhow? Anyone could just walk in here and do anything with me that they wanted to, and it would be my fault."

"Hey, God damn it, you didn't make the fucking payments and they repossessed YOUR fucking car." Clearly she didn't have me where she wanted me yet.

Mary was standing by the sink at the time of this conversation doing something that after all of this time escapes me. Suddenly she whipped around like a cornered predator and there was a kitchen knife in her hand. I could actually hear the blade make a swishing noise as it was jabbed at my stomach, only to instantly reverse course and make another "stab at it."

Now here's the thing that still amazes me to this day: I caught Mary's arm on the return trip, took the knife out of her hand, and laid it on the counter, all in mid-sentence. I never even broke cadence.

The incident was never even addressed.

The screaming match continued like the murder attempt was no more important than a fruit fly that might have flown between us at that same moment.

The uncontrolled cutlery started flying sometime in the later part of the morning, and the rest of the cage match happened like most of the rest. I remember standing right in the same spot in the kitchen. The sun rolled across the sky and I watched the shadows in the room move across the walls like the shadows in a turning airliner, just as I had in all of our arguments. Mary fixed herself lunch and ate it while I was berated. The kids came home from school, and were fixed dinner while I tried to agree my way, unsuccessfully, through the endless reminders of past indiscretions.

The family ate while I stood there fielding hot insults slammed off the bat of Mary's righteous indignation. I knew better than to even consider sitting down to eat. I had made that mistake before and the world fell on my head. I mean, in how many more ways could I show Mary that I just didn't care than by "casually" eating while her world was falling apart? Soon, Mary was asking the kids to join her in the Olympic style shit-flinging contest. She rehashed any time they had been grounded, yelled at, or in any kind of trouble, and the kids were encouraged to let me know just how big a prick they thought I was for it.

They did a pretty good job of it too.

Dinner dishes were cleaned off the table, visions of hurt feeling danced on the walls, pots were scrubbed, venom hung off oaths like green slime from Ghost Busters, the kids went off to wherever kids used to go off to in the 80's, and I stood there wondering how long this one was going to last. Mary moved off into the living room so she could catch up on some Capa De Monti horse shit from QVC, and I followed dutifully behind, apologizing for ever forcing her to have an affair, or for forcing her to leave her husband, who, incidentally was a real man because he had a real job in construction, and worked with his hands like a real man.

Soon we moved off to the fact that my penis clearly was substandard, and as if that wasn't bad enough I obviously had no idea how to use it. After all, she had had men bend her like a pretzel, and make her wait for it, and bang her real hard in the ass, and force her to jerk them off. After a while of this particular stage, I started to realize that this last diatribe was a multifaceted diamond of psychotic perfection that was designed to give me ideas to be used later . . . much later . . . in bed, while at the same time letting me know just how small a piece of crap I was. Additionally, she was letting me know just how much she had been sought after before me, (and apparently during me) . . . AND I think she got off on spitting all that premarital sexual crap into my unemotional face.

The sun was down and the street lights were on and we were still at it. Mary had moved off to the bathroom so she could get ready for bed and the bitch barrage turned back to the repossessed car. I knew beyond a shadow of a doubt that this was about to get real ugly because anytime we went all the way around the world on our loony-toon driven, supersonic jet, and ended back at the same point from where we started, that she was winding up for a real winner.

"Look," I said plainly, "it wasn't stolen. It was repossessed because you didn't make the payments."

POW . . . Mary hit me right in the nuts. I doubled over and fought the overwhelming desire to puke right there.

She cocked her fist back, and made ready for another

unchecked testicular assault.

I jumped back.

Mary got a look on her face like I had just called her a worthless cunt.

"You piece of shit!" she screamed "Look at you! Always making sure that you protect yourself! To hell with me and my feelings! Just make sure that nothing hurts you!"

As if to check to see if I was paying attention, Mary hauled off and gave me a full power, fact finding probe to the balls. I just stood there and kept my face as expressionless as I possibly could. Then POW, POW, POW, POW, four more times in rapid succession. Luckily it was dark so I was able to deftly move slightly to one side as the last two landed on my thigh.

Just that quickly, her demeanor totally changed. She instantly went from complete whacked out nut job that was clearly capable of ANY type of violence, to a pleading, vulnerable little girl.

"What do I have to do to get you to act like you care?" she said, almost begging. "To act like I'm anything at all to you? Do you have any idea what it makes me feel like when I have to treat you like that, when you make me have to hit you, and call you those names, and you don't even give a shit."

"I know sweetheart, I—" was all I got out.

"Well, then if you fucking know so much, then why don't you fucking change it? You pitiful pile of shit!" The nut was back in the house.

That was when she stalked off into the bedroom, slammed, and locked the door.

I knew what was coming next because this wasn't my first rodeo, and I knew exactly what was waiting in chute number four. A raging, hump back, pissed off Brahma Bull full of crazy. At this point—well at any point actually—but definitely at this point, there was nothing that I could do that would be the right thing. If I went into the bedroom to console her, then I would be labeled an asshole for continuing to push my "craziness" on her. If I left her alone, I would be an uncaring, unfeeling bastard.

As I pondered which path to take, and they had both been well traveled, Mary came storming back out of the bedroom, stomped into the kitchen, opened a bottle of wine, grabbed a glass, and started off for the bedroom again.

"Sweetheart . . ." I started to say, not really knowing what I was going to follow it up with.

Mary stopped and spun around, pointing at me with the bottle. "Don't you fucking dare," she growled.

She stood there for a few seconds holding me in her predatory glare, then she snorted her disgust and stomped off to see how fast she could get her system to infuse alcohol.

I couldn't foresee every last little detail of what the rest of the night was going to hold, but I didn't have to have a degree in nuclear physics to know that at some point there was going to be a lot of screaming, breaking things (on me or in the house), all of my clothes would be flung out in the front yard, and I would be told to get the hell out or Mary would call the police and tell them I had beaten her.

After a surprisingly short amount of time, I could hear Mary drunkenly talking to herself in the bedroom. It's funny, when you have to choose between jumping in a pit of snakes or a pool of sharks and there are no other choices, decision making becomes simple.

I walked into the bedroom.

Mary was lying on the bed, and had clearly passed "tipsy," proceeded directly to "shit faced" and most likely collected $200.

"Look—" I started.

"Shut the fuck up!" she cut me off.

"I'm sorry that I drove you to this." I had enough practice at this to know at least where I had to start, but apparently not enough experience to realize that the outcome would be the same no matter what I did. I would have been better off to just punch myself in the mouth, fling my belongings in the front yard, then go and sleep in my car.

"That's the first intelligent thing that you've said all night. You're sorry!"

To insinuate that I remember everything, or for that matter, anything that was said after that would be a complete fabrication. The conversation, if that's what it could be called, was a swirling putrid mess of complaints and accusations that I attempted to parry and thrust my way through. The list of grievances would start off in one direction then jerk off in another so fast that I was surprised I didn't need a cervical collar afterwards.

I remember that Mary punched me in the head once and I took it like she had just asked me what I wanted for dinner. I knew better than to "hurt her feelings" by showing any emotion to being clobbered in the head or even attempting to fend off the well telegraphed round house. Then she pushed me backwards through the bedroom door and I tripped over some piece of furniture.

"Oh yeah," she said sarcastically, "fall down like the little pussy that you are and try to make it look like I pushed you."

"You did push me," I said flatly. I was near the end of my rope and was dangerously close to not giving a shit what happened next.

"You worthless piece of shit," she said threateningly. "Get out! Get your shit and get the fuck out of my house!"

"I'm not going any place, and you don't really want me to."

Now, I realize that this last little jewel out of my mouth might have seemed ill advised. But in actuality it stemmed from another fight Mary and I had when she was telling me that one of the things that made her crazy when we fought was the fact that I did what she demanded I do. Apparently, she was telling me that it would show her that I cared if I knew that she didn't really want me to do what she was screaming at me to do.

Apparently I had misunderstood what she wanted.

"Oh really," she said, "you're not going anyplace, and I don't really want you to?"

She disappeared into our bedroom and came back out carrying an armload of my things that were soon decorating our front lawn. Back she went, and out the front door went another armload of clothing. Mary stopped and stood in the doorway pointing back out into the yard.

"Now get the fuck out of my house or I'm calling the cops."

I walked out the front door and started collecting my things as she stood there with her arms folded. I walked over to my car, opened the hatch back and threw them in.

"Go on," she said, "go on and run away. It's the only thing that you're good at, and it's what you always do anyway."

I turned around to face her, knowing that this was only what she was saying right now. No matter what I did, go, stay, argue, stay quiet, beg, demand, whatever, it was only going to infuriate her. Just as I knew that if I stayed it would make her even angrier, and if I left it would have the same effect.

"We don't have to do this," I said weakly. At that point I didn't want to go or stay, and I knew nothing I did was going to make any difference. I just wanted to die and get this over with.

"Get the fuck out!" she screamed.

I got in the car and waited to see what would happen next. Sometimes when we played this act out, Mary would just stalk off into the house. Sometimes she would throw things at the car as I backed out of the drive way. Sometimes she would scream that she couldn't believe I was a big enough piece of shit to leave.

Thank God this night was a stalk off into the house night.

Once again I found myself driving off into the night trying to figure out just what I could have done to make things turn out differently. Still, even at this point I knew that if I just found that *one* thing that was the key, I could turn all of this around and things would be alright.

As always, after I had been kicked out, I drove to a nearby gas station, parked in the back near a dumpster and tried to get some sleep. And, as usual, I left the doors unlocked in hopes that someone would try to rob me, and with any real luck I would be shot and mercifully killed during the robbery attempt.

I don't know how long I had been there, I only know that it was still dark and I must have dozed off because the incessant knocking on the driver's side window scared the hell out of me. In a

169

fog, I rolled the window down and realized that the visitor was one of Mary's kids telling me that I had to get back home because Mary was really drunk and she might hurt herself.

When I got back to the house, Mary was lying in the bed covered in her own vomit, and mumbling to herself about her father trying to have sex with her. I picked her up and set her in a chair in the bedroom, changed the bed clothes, and put her back in it. Then she puked all over everything again and I repeated the process.

The sun was coming up and there were things that needed to be done around the house. I let Mary sleep, and after she got up, I nursed her hangover.

It was like the night before had never even happened.

* * *

I found myself daydreaming after every two or three sentences as I wrote this last chapter thinking, "I should have done this, or I should have said that." Sometimes I became lost in thought, reliving each and every intimate detail, whishing that I could somehow go back in time and live these episodes over again. But then I think, "Would I be able to change anything? Or would I just be sucked back into that vortex of unreasonableness and find myself wallowing in a quagmire of misery all over again?" I tell myself that I would never let that happen again, that I'm a different person now and I have regained my self-respect. But deep inside, I know that I had self-respect before I met Mary and in essence I have just rebuilt myself to back to the person I was before her.

It has taken me four months to write the last three pages. When the above incident took place, Prince was an up and coming rock star, not even coming close to having the ego it would take to think of himself as a symbol instead of having a name. As I dredge up the screamingly painful emotions of the past, it is the most amazing thing to me that I ever extricated myself from that mess in the first place.

It's raining today and my horses are calmly grazing in the pasture and I watch them from my porch as I write today's helping of painful memories. I'll hold on to this pastoral scene as I press on for the silently abused.

TWENTY-TWO

As I said before, Mary and I had bought our first house together just before the cage match that I mentioned above. My credit score by now was about the same number as my age since by then we had been sued by about fifteen different companies for delinquent bills. All four of our credit cards were maxed out, we didn't have a savings or checking account because of the evil plan the banks had exacted on us to steal what was rightfully theirs in the first place, and I didn't have three cents to put down on a new home, let alone 10%. BUT, I had served in the military for four glorious years near the end of the Vietnam War and I was eligible for a zero money down, low interest mortgage from the VA.

The house we bought was a three bedroom, two bath, ranch house that was still under construction in a fairly large development about fifteen miles farther away from work than I already was. We paid an unbelievable $74,000, and it was one of the biggest models that the developer offered. Unfortunately, as a friend of mine would later so eloquently put it, if you by in a $70,000 neighborhood your buying into neighbors with a $70,000 mentality. The sad part is that for my little band of miscreants, this $70,000 mentality was a step up. I swear to God, every morning my alarm clock should have been the theme song to "Cops."

Mary knew that we were movin' on up as well and she handled that with all the dignity and grace that I had come to expect from her over the years. She picked a fight with every single family that lived anywhere near us, just to show them that they weren't any better than us. Then combine that with her hysterical hatred of all women and unfavorable knowledge that the only women that I didn't want to screw were the ones that I hadn't met yet, and life was a veritable cornucopia of stuff that would make today's reality shows look like a sermon in a Methodist church.

I guess that for simplicity's sake I can break things into a few different groups, because we had different problems with different neighbors that kept the local police department busy for years.

Let me start with the people that lived on our left side. These people were a young couple that was just starting out. They seemed to be pleasant enough (strike one), I can't remember now if they had one or two boys (strike two—Mary had a hysterectomy before we met and we couldn't have any more children), and the wife was young and attractive (strike three . . . and the side retires!).

After this many years, I can't remember what one incident started the hardship between our two families. I remember that the husband had supposedly made a pass at Mary while I was at work, and I hadn't responded properly by killing his dog or beating the shit out of one of his pre-school kids or something. Actually, I knew that the accusation was a lie because if he had in fact made any kind of even halfhearted attempt to get into Mary's skivvies he would have been successful and I would have instantly known about it.

At any rate the fight was on.

Think "Judge Judy" or "People's Court" and all of the trite moronic things people drag each other into court for and that was what my life had turned into. Their dog would come into our yard and a fight would start. Our dog would go into their yard and a fight would start. Eventually the yelling over the fence escalated into scattered periods of pushing and shoving, and the cops were thrown into the mix.

I used to sit in the middle of that vortex of bullshit while these poor officers of the law would try to mediate the unmediateable and think, "Man . . . I wouldn't have your job for a million dollars," because I was sure that for every one of me they had to deal with, there were 1000 more assholes just waiting to for a chance to act like a spoiled child to the poe poe.

My clever ruse of keeping Mary separated from my job for the sake of security left one small opening that there was no way I could head off. If Mary happened to *call* me at work, (pre cell phones) and a woman answered, I was screwed. The fact that management usually answered the phones and the government agency I worked for was sadly devoid of women in management helped. However, if Mary should call and hear a female voice working in the background or coming from another facility over one of the open speakers in the room, I would never be able to talk my way out of that one.

Consequently, every time the phone rang at the managers' desk I would jump out of my skin and start counting the number of holes in my story that were currently in the room with me. It was very distracting. So the fact that a man answered the phone the day Mary called to tell me she had been in a fist fight with the woman next door, and the cops were on the way was a life saver. The fact that Mary was hysterical when she called and wouldn't have noticed the Normandy landing in the background was gravy.

I got off the phone, talked my boss into letting me take leave and raced home as fast as I could. As I look back on it, I have no idea why I was in such a hurry. I knew that whatever had happened was ignorant, and childish, and when I got there I was just going to be expected to support actions that I knew in my heart were clearly out of line. But the other thing I knew was that after the dust settled, and the cops left, and all the spectators went back in there houses I was going to have to deal with whatever Mary had perceived to have happened. And if her perception was that I had done anything less than back her 100%, there was going to be hell to pay.

I got home before the police arrived on the scene. I guess they recognized the address and decided to prioritize, putting the rescue of cats from trees and cleaning their gun in front of going out to the nuthouse once again to deal with very tall two year olds. Mary was livid and the kids were all jerked out of shape as well. I never got the entire story . . . not because of time constraints; I never got the full story period. That might get in the way of Mary's agenda.

From what I could gather, at some point the woman next door was walking up her driveway when Mary or one of the kids made some smart-ass comment. The fact that in most people's eyes this would make the argument *our fault* was lost on Mary and her children. They actually thought that they could say or do anything they wanted, to anyone they wanted and there should be no retaliation.

At some point, the woman either came back out of the house, or never actually got inside, but punches were thrown. Some were thrown between Mary and the woman and still others were thrown between Mary's daughter and the woman. At any rate, as I'm having the story told to me, there came an authoritarian knock of great demand at my door.

To say the least, the cop that was standing in my doorway was not amused.

The more that I related the story to him, the more he came to the realization that I wasn't even there for the incident. So he started to get the story from Mary. I could see that this was going to come to a disastrous end. Either I was going to get the shit beaten out of me after the cops left for letting them talk *that* way to Mary, or I was going to get the shit beaten out of me for not supporting the line of convoluted crap that she was laying out for the cop. So I kept trying to interject sanity into the conversation. After a few minutes, the cop asked me to step out in the street with him.

Once I got out there, I realized that the husband from next door was already in the street, apparently waiting for us.

"You two seem to be the only near rational people involved here," the cop said to me over his shoulder. "Maybe we can get something worked out if the two of you talk and come to an understanding." Then he stopped, turned around and pointed his finger in my face. "Because this shit has to stop before someone gets hurt or goes to jail," he said.

Once he got us together, he started playing mediator. I have to say, this guy was good. Even though I was certain that after this little "come to Jesus" meeting was over, I was totally screwed. I had no choice but to let my rational side show through. Unfortunately, the cop had made one horrible error in judgment. He had allowed his partner, who was clearly agitated with the entire childish affair to stay down in the street with us. In hindsight it would have been much better if one of the two of them had stayed up at my house to ensure that no one came out of my front door.

At some point in the conversation I was having, the neighbor guy had stepped out of the street and was standing about six inches inside my yard on my grass.

"Tell that asshole to stay out of our yard," Mary yelled from the front porch.

The cop was in the middle of making some point and stopped in mid-sentence. The neighbor guy started stomping around in little circles in the grass yelling, "Holy shit, I'm in your yard! Holy shit, I'm in your yard!"

"You see? You see what that jerk does?" Mary yelled "Arrest his stupid ass! I don't have to put up with that shit!"

I just stood there looking at the ground wishing that a giant hole would open up and swallow me right there, never to be seen again. I actually considered trying to jerk the cop's gun out of his holster forcing him to shoot me.

"Fuck this," the cop's partner said. "How long are you going to stand here and take this bullshit before you let me take one of these jack-offs to jail?"

"You're right," the cop said dejectedly. It was obvious that this guy really wanted to fix the problem, and it was plain to see that it most certainly wasn't going to happen. "We're leaving now," he said to both of us. "If anybody comes back out here tonight a shitload of people are going straight to jail."

Neither of us said anything. I think we both felt like a couple of dumb asses. Mary saw the cops leaving and started yelling at me. "That's it?" She screamed "That asshole gets to do whatever he wants and you're not going to make them do anything about it."

I knew right at that point that I was screwed no matter what I did. If I just went back in the house like I should have done Mary would go ballistic. If I confronted the cops OR the neighbor I was going to spend the night in the comfortable confines of the local jail.

Jail sounded pretty good to me right then.

I walked up to the surly partner as he was walking past my car and put my hand up.

"Hey—" was all I got out. I have never had my arm jerked up behind my back that fast before . . . or since. Instantly, I was bent over the trunk of my car and pain was shooting through my shoulder.

"Is there something you feel needs to be added to this monkey fuck?" the cop asked directly into my ear.

"Nope, can't think of a thing," I said out of the side of my squished up face.

"Funny," he said, still holding my head to the trunk lid,

"almost sounded to me like you might have had something you wanted to say."

"Just wanted to say have a nice night, officer."

"Thanks," he said releasing me just as fast as he had jacked my arm up. He leaned in to my face so close that our noses almost touched. "You have a nice night too."

When I got back in the house Mary was livid, and I knew at the very least it was going to a very long night, but most likely a very long several days.

Naturally the fight started the same way that it always did. "If you cared about me you wouldn't let anyone abuse me like that . . . ." Blah, blah, blah, yadda, yadda, yadda. And to be perfectly honest, I couldn't even begin to tell you specifics about how the rest of it went. I remember that it went on nonstop for at least two and a half days, there was one halfhearted knifing attempt made by Mary that, as usual, I easily deflected. But the biggest thing I remember is that was the night she broke my nose.

She caught me off guard in the dark with a vicious right hook that came out of nowhere while she was in mid-sentence. One minute I was standing there agreeing that I was a worthless, gay, shit bag, and the next I was seeing stars, my eye were tearing up, and my nose was bleeding. I kept trying to sniff the blood back down my throat so Mary wouldn't see it and go nuts because I forced her to hit me like that. When she heard the sniffing, she went nuts anyway because I was such a pussy that I was crying instead of taking care of her needs.

The funny part is that I had no idea that she had broken my nose until a few years later. After I had left her, I had a pretty serious motorcycle accident. The X-rays showed a broken nose and a few other injuries that I had received at Mary's hand. The doctor told me that I had to slow down and start acting my age . . . assuming that they had all come from motorcycle accidents. By then, I had already learned to protect myself from ridicule.

I told him I would ride safer in the future.

Naturally, this wouldn't be the last incident that we would become embroiled in with that particular pair of neighbors. For reasons that would only make sense to Mary, she had seen one of the two little boys from that house walking up their driveway alone, so she took that opportunity to go over and tell him that his daddy wasn't really his daddy and he should ask his mommy who his daddy really was.

I had never seen anything like that before, or since. She sees this kid in the front yard, nobody else is around, and just like that she comes up with a heinous plan like that. And as if the fact that she thought that way wasn't bad enough, she had no problem what so ever with telling a little four- or five-year-old kid something like that.

Of course the cops were called and we all ended up standing out in the front yard while local law enforcement dealt with our bullshit. Sometimes I would imagine that while we were all standing around acting like impetuous three year olds being babysat by at least three squad cars, the real criminals were having a field day looting and pillaging.

I guess eventually cops—or certain cops—got tired of jerking around with us and decided to take matters into their own hands. I was hanging ceiling fans on the back porch when Mary came running through the glass sliding doors nearly knocking me off the ladder.

"Some jerk from next door is parked in our front yard," she said, out of breath.

I knew that this was the beginning of another round of "cops" and I was simply going along for the ride. After all, some low life subhuman was actually parked on the blessed, virginal grass that surrounded our fortress- like castle. And like all escapees from America's lower, middle class, someone being in our yard, worse yet parked on our lawn, was punishable by death or dismemberment. After all, by God, that was our *property* and them folks was *trespassin'*. I walked out the front door and, sure enough a white crown Victoria was parked parallel to the street, on my grass, right next to my mail box.

I was pissed.

Not pissed because someone was parked on my lawn. I honestly didn't care if gremlins were doing doughnuts in tiny little jeeps all over my grass while their relatives corn holed my dog. I really had bigger fish to fry than that. The thing that pissed me off was the fact that some jerk had just given Mary all the ammunition she needed for a good old fashion donnybrook that I was supposed to put an end to and prove, once again, that I really loved her.

I walked out to the car to see if anyone was inside. The windows were tinted fairly dark and you really couldn't see inside.

As I walked up to the car a man came around the fence that divided our precious front yard from the neighbors and walked over to the driver's door of the crown vic.

"Why are you parked in my front yard?" I asked.

"I'll only be here a minute," the man said offhandedly as he retrieved something from the front seat and started to walk away.

I looked over at the empty driveway in front of the house he was on his way back to, and it dawned on me that this was some jack off friend of the guy that we had been fighting with, and he was actually TRYING to incite an argument.

"Hey," I yelled after him "get your mother fucking piece of shit car out of my God Dammed yard."

He stopped and turned around, "I'll only be a minute," he said smiling.

"Not a minute you fuck head!" I had gone from just wanting someone...or something to kill me to wanting desperately to do bodily harm to someone else. I knew better than to go over and confront anyone because that was obviously just what they wanted. Then as I stood there trying to decide what to do next, and being apparently unable to come up with the correct idea of going back in

185

my house and ignoring the jerk off benignly parked in my yard, I saw this guy and the neighbor peeking over the fence at me.

That successfully stripped away the last vestiges of intelligent thought. I should have recognized this fact when I stormed into the house hell bent on revenge. Mary stopped me and told me not to do anything stupid. The fact that a total lunatic was telling ME to settle down should have been a clue that I was out of control.

Luckily, instead of getting the sledge hammer out of the garage like I planned to do I picked up the phone and called the police. Then I stormed around the house waiting for my mediators to show up. In a few minutes I received a call from the police department telling me that they had a police operation being conducted in my area and the car parked in my front yard was possibly an un-marked squad car.

I lost my mind again. Living with this bundle of insecurity called a wife wasn't enough. Now I had the police department trying to start a neighborhood fight when there wasn't one so they could arrest me. I walked into the kitchen and grabbed a handful of eggs from the refrigerator. I had a pretty good arm back then so I was able to launch my eggs of indignation from the confines of the entry way to my house. Consequently I knew there wouldn't be a dashboard video of me egging a cop car.

Apparently, Dick Tracy saw the eggs hitting the side of his car and he came bounding down the street.

"Your credibility is shot in the ass!" He was yelling at me. "Your credibility is over!"

"How about if you just drive your ass back to the station," I said smiling from my doorway "and tell your boss how you got your car egged while you were trying to incite a neighborhood riot on your off time for no reason."

He tore up a good 10 feet of my yard as he took off down the road.

It was worth it.

Those poor people living in there very first house, that just happened to be unlucky enough to have moved in next to us lasted for a few more months, and a few more fights until they couldn't take it anymore. They sold their house for next to nothing and moved on. I feel sure that they have post traumatic effects of the time they spent dealing with that lunacy that still manifests itself to this day. After I ran away and hid from my abuser…and that's exactly what I did…I tried to find that family so I could personally apologize for the hurt that I had caused them and ask for forgiveness. I was unsuccessful, but I hope if they happen to read this they will accept my heart felt pain and sorrow for what they had to endure at my hand.

The family that lived on the other side of us was another thing all together.

After I got to know them it became obvious that they had crawled out of the same swamp of hate filled feuding that my wife had come from. This would become a real Hatfield and McCoy episode that would eventually end in gun play.

I don't remember what the first fight was that brought our two families together. It was the same type of crap that we were dealing out to the people on the other side of us, and it was during the same time frame, but the particulars are lost to the years. Of course there was the obligatory yelling, name calling, and threats made across a property line. Naturally the police were involved and they took notes on the complaints that were tossed around like confetti on New Year's Eve while they stood there with a Joe Friday air of indifference.

Then one day while I was at work one of the people from that family told Mary that the good thing about our houses being so far apart was that if ours were to burn down it probably wouldn't effect theirs at all. Supposedly there was also some comment made that it would be really unfortunate if one of our pets got poisoned. There was a lot of that going around you know, and you never really knew who you could trust and who had it in for you.

I was certain that these things actually had been said and it wasn't just made up because it had an amazing effect on Mary. It seemed that she had finally met her match and she was scared shitless because of it. Naturally Mary retaliated in a way that she was expert at.

Subterfuge.

The couple that lived across the street from our neighbors were in the Air Force, had no children, seemed friendly enough, and had no idea what they were living around. They had just finished building a fence around their back yard and the husband had ill-advisedly mentioned to Mary that he hadn't bothered to get a building permit. Within a few days Mary called the county permit office and told them that a person in her neighborhood had erected a fence without permission. When the county asked if she would be willing to give her name and address for the complaint she indicated that she would be glad to, and furnished the name and address of the Hatfield's next door. Then just to round out the evil plan she told the people that she had just turned in to the county that she had overheard a rumor that the Hatfield's were the ones that turned them in.

Every time this poor guy farted "the Hatfields" turned him in. The one thing that Mary hadn't counted on was the fact that the guy she kept busting was intelligent, and adult enough to go across the street and ask the Hatfields why they had a personal vendetta against him. I don't know what was said between them but I guess that Mr. Hatfield was able to convince fence guy that it wasn't him that had busted him. And it also seems that Mr. Hatfield was pretty good at math, because shortly after he put 2 and 2 together we started getting clobbered by the county.

No permit for a fence.

No Permit for and above ground pool.

No dog license.

That was when Mr. Hatfield decided to run a fence from his back yard, past our house and all the way out to the street. I thought that was great because if Mary couldn't see what was going on out there then maybe she would settle down about them at least and just go back to making my life miserable.

Instead, this new fence threw Mary into an absolute rage. I think that what really set her off was that Hatfield had hired a fence company to build the fence for him so clearly there was a building permit. The day construction started on the fence Mary was inconsolable. When I got home from work she and the oldest boy were cooking up a plan to wait until dark then go out and push all the fence posts over. This may not seem like a big deal but these poor guys had been working in 95 degree heat all day, and all of these posts, about 15 of them, were set in concrete. Consequently, when the workers came back the next day every post would have to be pulled up, the concrete dug out or new post holes dug, and then each post would have to be reset.

So I said instead of doing all of that we should just take two of them out of the ground next to our house so no one could see us and Mary could still get her point across. Naturally Mary was pissed off at me, mentioning once or twice that I was a pussy, and if I thought anything of her then I would be glad to destroy our neighbor's fence for no reason at all other than placating her. Fortunately her son was the voice of reason in this case and Mary acquiesced to stealing two fence posts.

And that is just how things were shortly after sunset when the police showed up at the neighbor's house with three squad cars…for two stolen fence posts. Apparently we were beginning to get a reputation with the police department. When I saw the flashing lights blue lights reflecting off the houses across the street I knew that I had better do something with the two 4X4X8 pieces of "evidence" that were sitting in my garage. So while the cops got the Hatfield's version of what went down I busied myself with cutting the posts into manageable sections so I could stick them in my attic.

I can tell you right now that I felt like total shit for my part in this ignorance. It was my idea to take the posts out in the first place. I had to take personal responsibility for that, but there was no way that the police or the court system was going to care that the only reason I let it happen in the first place was so that a much more destructive plan wouldn't be exacted on the neighborhood. Naturally there was no point in telling the cops any of this because they wanted to put one or all of us in jail so bad they could taste it. Besides that, if I came clean with the police the best outcome would be that my life would be hell at home, and most likely in serious jeopardy.

Before long the inevitable knock came at our front door and three uniformed officers of the law stood on my front porch all wearing identical "would you give us a fucking break" looks on their faces. They wanted to hear my side of the story, and obviously I had no side because I hadn't done anything. They seemed to accept that explanation and were all ready to go when one of the female cops turned around and asked if she could look in my garage. The only reason that I mention her gender is because every cop out there gave a look like she was being a pain in the ass. I knew there was nothing in the garage so I went out there with them and opened the door.

"You know," she said looking at the floor "it's funny. It's late, and when we pull up I can hear you running power tools out here with the door shut. Now, I think that's odd because it's still about 85 degrees out here, and the humidity is at least 80%, and I'm thinking' 'who the hell would be doing wood working out here this late with the door shut'. And now I see saw dust all over the place and not a stick of wood to be seen. How do you explain that?"

I don't remember what line of pure bullshit I fed her. I only remember that it was bullshit.

"Mmmmmmm, Hmmmmmmm." she said like she was my mother "I'll be right back."

She walked down to the sidewalk to have a conference with the sergeant that was ring master for that night's entertainment. There was a lot of exaggerated hand gesturing and exasperated looks exchanged between the two, and I remember thinking that the only thing I had going for me right then was the fact that none of these good ole' boy cops wanted to hear anything the short black woman in police cloths had to say.

The fact that she had my dumb ass dead to rights was blissfully irrelevant to them. Unfortunately for me she took the time that was necessary to not back down, and continued to push her point of view.

And that was how I got arrested for malicious mischief…

The cops didn't lead me away in handcuffs and toss me in a cage with mother rapiers and father stabbers, or even make me sit on the group W bench. They simply read me my rights, told me that I was being arrested, what I was being arrested for, and that I would be released on my own resonances.

I hired a lawyer that told me there was no way that the DA was going to prosecute a case a flimsy as this one, and that I had nothing to worry about. So I guess he was mildly surprised when my court date came around. I don't remember any of the intricacies of the trial, all I remember is my attorney asking the Hatfields if they had paid for the fence at the time of the incident. When they told him they hadn't my lawyer said that the fence in question did not yet belong to the Hatfields and in fact still belonged to the fence company. Consequently the Hatfields had no right to bring charges against me regarding property that didn't belong to them. If anyone wanted to prosecute me it would have to be the fence company.

The judge agreed and the case was thrown out of court. I half expected the Hatfields to be waiting on the courthouse steps with shot guns after the trial so they could seek retribution right there. Honestly I wouldn't have blamed them.

…the gun play? Well that happened after the hurricane tried to kill us all and that's for a later chapter. So keep reading.

TWENTY THREE:

As I said before we were always living from paycheck to paycheck. Mary could make sure money passed through our house faster than water ran through a bottomless bucket. She and the kids always had very nice cloths. The house was filled with an endless parade of cheap...but constantly replaced...furniture, wicker fans, giant terra cotta vases, and electronics. Mary had an ongoing relationship with QVC, HSN, and a company called Fingerhut that sold the cheapest of needless shit to idiots.

Mary needed to replace her repossessed car so naturally, being a stay at home mom that had three kids to take care of and a house to run she bought a "buy here pay here" Pontiac Fiero. For those of you that are not into cars the Fiero is a mid-engine, 2 seat, plastic piece of crap that is about as big as a go-kart and barely stayed together when it was brand new. I had a "buy here pay here" Mazda GLC that had pulled a cannon with Sherman on his infamous march to the sea, and one of the kids had a drivers license now so I had to by him one overly financed "buy here pay here" POS after another because he kept wrecking cars like it was his life's ambition.

I realize that many of you may have been sheltered enough in life that you would not immediately know what a "buy here pay here" car is. Some used car dealerships know that there is a section of America out there that may be less than flush when it comes to liquid cash on hand. But, just like the wonder of a sanctioned loan shark like a check cashing store, these dealerships have filed the necessary paper work to allow them to sell you a car, and let you make payments directly to them. These are 100% profit businesses that buy crappy cars for next to nothing and make them just barely operable. When they put them out on the lot the down payment to buy these cars is the full amount of whatever they initially paid for them in the first place. Consequently, the day of the sale they have already made their money back and any money that they might get in the form of monthly payments is gravy. The instant that a payment is missed the car is reposed and the process starts all over again.

Mary never did anything for the household while I was at work. When I got home, or on my day off we would go to the grocery store, or get money orders to pay the bills, or whatever errands needed to be done. As I've said earlier, when I would try to get the kids to help with house/yard work they would bitch to Mary and we would all have a "what a jerk dad is" meeting. Sometimes these meetings would go on all day as I sat there and listened to how I was abusive because I wanted them to cut the grass, clean their rooms, or take out the trash. We're not talking about toddlers here, these kids were in high school.

Eventually I just gave up and did everything myself. Sometimes a car would breakdown and I would be out in the driveway fixing it until 1 or 2 in the morning. Then I would get up at 5AM so I could be to work by 6. Mary constantly wanted our brand new house remolded and since we had no money I did the work myself. All of the windows were taken out. The walls underneath them were knocked out and I replaced them with wooden French Doors. I lost count of how many decks I built...tore down...and rebuilt trying to keep her happy.

Ceiling fans galore sprouted from our inverted popcorned ceiling fan field. Constant painting inside and out of the house every time that Mary had a change of mood and wanted more...or less color in her life. Sealing the driveway, building concrete flower boxes, and landscaping were a nonstop nightmare that Wes Craven couldn't have kept up with. And all of this was on top of normal household chores like cutting the grass and washing the cars. Then I would work 40 hours a week. Sleep deprivation and sensory overload just like in POW camps. The only difference was that the food was a little better. After a few months of this you had no idea who you were or what you were doing.

By that time I had been living like this for 8 years.

Mary wanted a built in pool but there was no way we could afford something like that. Naturally a giant fight followed and I was told that if I really loved her and cared at all about the hell I had put her through (???) I would find a way to make it happen. I knew you couldn't get blood out of a turnip, and there was nowhere else to get money or financing. But, as Mary pointed out, there was one option.

Sears had a 15X30 foot above ground pool that we could "afford". All I had to do was dig a hole in the back yard and set the pool in it. It's amazing to me when I look back on this because I never even thought that digging a 20X35 foot wide; three foot deep hole in my back yard using nothing but a steel pry bar and a shovel was the least bit crazy. Mary wanted it...I couldn't afford to do it any other way...so it was going to happen.

The hole became my life. When I wasn't working or fighting with Mary I was digging my hole. Every day, day in and day out I would dig. When I worked the day shift I would dig until well after dark with the aid of work lights I set up. When I worked the night shift I would jump in the hole first thing in the morning and work until I left for work. I never once considered the insanity of it, or the seemingly Sisyphean implications. All I knew or cared about was that all of the time I spent in that ever expanding hole was time that I wasn't going to have to spend around the other craziness in my life.

After a short time my hole started to take on "Great Escape" like qualities. I had no place to put my dirt. I guess I could have filled my pants legs with it then walked around the neighborhood as I slowly let then dirt drop to the street, but Commandant Mary would never allow me to walk around the neighborhood by myself. After all, any second that I was left on my own would be time that I was having an affair.

I began pilling the dirt up around the side of the hole, and that was working out great. The more dirt I piled up the deeper the hole got without having to actually dig more. But after a short time I ran out of yard to pile the dirt up in. After all the pool was taking up two thirds of the yard and I might have been able to start using the fence as a retaining wall, but even in my limited mental capacity it seemed that this would come to no good in short order.

Eventually I started to hit giant lime rocks. This was a mixed blessing in that I could move a larger amount of hole filler all at once, but getting those big bastards out of the hole was going to present a problem. The only way that I could see to fix it was build a little dirt ramp at one end of the hole and force the boulders up it using the pry bar. Kind of the same way Egyptian slaves built the pyramids. It was really slow going and the 95 degree temperatures and 80% humidity wasn't helping at all. At six foot three I was down to about 165 pounds.

All day Mary would sit in the house and watch QVC, go out shopping, or write country western songs about what an abusive piece of shit I was. In the afternoon she would bring me something to drink, or come out with a wet wash cloth to wipe my forehead. From one minute to the next I had no idea who was coming out of that door, and I did everything I could to hide in my hole and maintain a low profile.

Out of site out of mind.

Eventually the hole was completed and it was time to erect the pool. I can tell you that trying to keep the outer wall up and fit it in the bottom track all by myself while always trying to keep the whole thing level was like trying to wrestle a 60 foot Anaconda while walking on a balance beam. Every now and then Mary would get bored sitting in the house and come out to start a fight just as I was at a point where I couldn't stop what I was doing. More than once I would be standing there holding three things in place at one time trying to answer pointed questions about things that I had done years before, or reassure her that I didn't have any of the negative feeling towards her that she thought I was displaying as far back as before we were married.

The fact that she would show up right at the worst possible time was never lost on me. I knew that she would sit in the house and watch me. As soon as I was completely engaged with the project she would come out and innocently start asking loaded questions. I knew that this wasn't just some sick way to screw with me for fun or even a power play to see if she could make me stop working. It was simply the fact I was completely absorbed in the project that I was working on and her insecurity was so crippling that she had to be reassured every minute that the pool wasn't more important to me than she was.

Eventually the pool was erected and since there was a five foot wide three foot deep trench all the way around it I had to build a deck to cover that. As an afterthought, the deck was a real life saver because I could leave all of those giant lime rocks under it and not have to find a place for them. The rest of the dirt was taken care of by lots of raised flower beds that I built out of concrete blocks covered with stucco.

The big day arrived as I shut the water off to the garden hose that had been filling the pool and I went into the house to bring Mary out to see what she thought.

"Can I walk on that deck without if falling in?" she asked darkly.

I knew I was screwed.

"Of course you can sweetheart," I said trying to lighten the mood. "You know me, if one nail is good then five are great."

She walked up on the deck and looked darkly into the pool like she was staring into the abyss.

"You're acting like this because you know this is junk aren't you," she said without looking up.

"I think it looks pretty good actually..." I said blankly. I didn't know where this was going but I knew it wasn't good.

"You know that there's a ton of trash under this deck and you don't even care." She turned around to face me. "And that's just fine with you isn't it, because this is for me. I bet that if that bitch you were dating before you met me wanted a pool like this there wouldn't be a bunch of trash under the deck would there."

"What trash are you talking about?"

"Isn't that just like you," she whined "treat me like shit and then defend yourself."

"I'm not defending myself; I just don't know what trash you're talking about."

"If you gave the least little shit about me you'd know exactly what trash I'm talking about. Day after day I would come out here and see the yard full of crap that you were collecting and I kept thinking 'I hope that he plans on doing something with this' but I knew that eventually you'd just hide it all under the deck."

"Are you talking about the dirt and rocks?"

"That's exactly what I'm talking about, and you know it! Now every time I sit on this deck or get in this pool I'm going to know that you didn't care enough about me to do it right in the first

205

place."

"You can't even see it…besides it's the same dirt and rock that's always been there. It was just under the grass before. Now it's under the deck and you still can't see it."

Mary stalked off into the house, and I drug myself along behind her. At least I would be able to take my lumps inside out of the view of the neighborhood.

"What did you want me to do with the dirt?" I said at Mary's back as she stalked off to the bedroom.

"It's not just the dirt," she spit "it's everything, it's our life, it's the way you treat me, it's how you show me every day that you just couldn't care less. If you cared about me at all that trash wouldn't be under the deck right now."

I know that at this point a normal person would have been thinking that they should get the hell out of this nut house, or that there was no way to win so just to hell with it. But the only thing I was thinking was that if I had just found someplace else to put the dirt and rocks none of this would be happening right now. I was also thinking that no matter what happened, or what I did in the future in regards to that pool it wasn't going to matter because all it was now was a giant water filled monument to the fact that I didn't love my wife enough to do it right the first time.

In the ensuing fight I tried to make it up to Mary by telling her that I would take the deck back down and try to find someplace to put all that rock and dirt, but that just made things worse. If I could take the time to find someplace for it now then why couldn't I care enough about her in the first place to find a place for it before I had to use it to screw her over one more time.

Naturally the insanity lasted through the night and into the next day. I called into work for sick leave so I could stay and slug it out without making her feel that my job was more important than fixing the fact that I had put the rocks under the deck just to hurt her. All that day I stood in the same spot while Mary told me what a worthless piece of shit I was. The kids went to school, came home, ate dinner, went to bed, and I was still standing there doing my level best to parry and thrust all of the accusations Mary hurled at me, as I tried to convince her that I really did love her.

I didn't love her of course. I didn't feel anything by this time. I was simply trying to keep my head above water and try to stay one step ahead of Mary's feeling of inadequacy. I was just trying to survive. The bad part is that I didn't even remember what I was trying to survive for. I had resigned myself long ago to the fact that this was going to be my life forever, until I was blissfully taken away from it by death, so I honestly don't know what I was TRYING to do. It was now just my way of life and I stumbled through it from one day to the next, meeting each new sunrise with all of the apathy of a cat watching the radio. I just didn't care.

That night as the screaming and defending reached its crescendo Mary got out of bed totally naked walked out into the front yard and closed the garage door then turned around and told me that if I cared about her at all I would have never let her walk out the front door naked. This was new even in my whacked out little corner of the world.

"Will you please get back in the house," I said.

"No, fuck you!" Mary screamed defiantly, arms folded across naked breasts.

"Look...please..." I said.

"You mother fucker!" Mary screamed. And she bounced into the house and slammed the door.

I was now in the shit or go blind mode. While I was standing there trying to decide what to do next Mary came flying back out of the house....dressed this time. Flung the garage door back open and got in her buy here, pay here Corvette. I was standing behind it when I saw the backup lights come on and I jumped out of the way just in time. The fender brushed the back of my hand and the stench of angrily burnt rubber filled my nose. The indignant red Corvette flew backwards into the street, hesitated for a second then seemed to actually stretch as every single horsepower under that hood was cattle prodded into action.

Mary's tail lights fishtailed around the corner and out of sight.

In a few seconds angry headlights lead a violent red Corvette around the corner at the other end of the street. Mary had raced around the short block and was inbound for round two. The Vette slid to a stop in a red smudge in front of the driveway I was standing in.

"You're not going to even do anything to stop this are you, you fucking pussy," Mary screamed indignantly through the open passenger window.

"Sweetheart, please just come back in the house so we can

talk about this," I pleaded.

Mary's face got even darker.

"That's it?" she said "That's all you have after everything you've done to me?"

The Corvette leapt from a standstill, mercilessly beat up the asphalt, slid around the corner and was gone.

For a few seconds.

The evil headlights appeared at the other end of the street again then screeched to a stop in front of me.

"I'm going down to the marina and drive this fucking car into the bay," Mary hissed through the still open passenger window. "What are you going to do about that, asshole?"

"Sweetheart, please," I begged as I squatted down next to the open window and put my hands on the sill.

"You pathetic peace of shit." The Vette was ticking with heat from the workout it was getting but still it obeyed as Mary slammed down on the accelerator taking a chunk out of my left hand with the door handle. I stood there bleeding as the tail lights made another maniacal trip around the corner.

Instantly, clawing headlights screamed around the corner,

rolled up into the driveway, and slammed to a stop. I squatted next to the window, hands off this time, and I could see Mary was crying in the driver's seat.

"Why don't you just get in the car with me," she sobbed.

What could go wrong there? At least she wasn't screaming anymore so I stood up with every intension of getting in the car.

"I just want to kill us both so we can spend eternity together," Mary said as I stood.

"Ah, what?"

"I've wanted that for a long time. I can't take the thought of you leaving me anymore you being with anybody else, and I just want to get this over with. So just get in the car and we can be together forever."

"What about the kids?" I said trying to defuse this lunacy.

"I don't care anymore."

Well we had that in common now.

"I would like nothing better than that," I lied "but we can't just leave the kids like that. Just come in the house and we can talk about this."

The tired Corvette gratefully slid into the garage. I closed the garage door, Mary got out of the car, walked into the house, got undressed, and got into bed. I spent the rest of the night reassuring her that if it weren't for the kids I would love to be killed with her and spend eternity together. The fairytale sent Mary off to sleep just in time for me to get a shower and go to work.

Two months later the irony train would pull into our little corner of paradise. One of the neighbors, I assume the Hatfields, called building and zoning. I had no idea I needed a building permit to set up a pool so I didn't have one. My penance would be to take down the pool, dismantle the deck and fill in the hole.

Now all the *trash* would be back under the grass and was acceptable again.

TWENTY FOUR:

Hurricanes are some of the most interesting weather phenomenon there are to observe…from afar. The ones that affect the East Coast of the United States generally begin as strong low pressure systems either in the Gulf of Mexico or off the western shores of North Africa. The African hurricanes gather strength in the form of moister and unstable air that is sucked up from the warm waters of the Atlantic Ocean in the southern latitudes as they lumber ever westward, jinking here and wobbling there, not unlike a running back trying to head fake a defensive linebacker. Hundreds, if not thousands of people are employed by the federal government just to study, watch, and warn the American people of an approaching storm.

As the storm approaches the east coast predictions are made as to where, or even if land fall of the hurricane eye will take place. For days residents of the possibly affected areas will plot the storms movement on charts that are given out by supermarkets hoping that when the inevitable run on canned goods and bottled water takes place they will remember where they got the tracking chart that saved their lives in the first place. As the storm draws closer and landfall predictions are refined people closest to the center of the predicted path will begin to move potential missiles out of yards. Ornamental vases, and planters that sit around pool decks are taken inside garages, lawn furniture is tossed into pools to keep it from blowing away, newbies to hurricane country will put crosses of masking tape on windows. The old timers know that all the masking tale will do is let the home owner know from a distance that the window is gone after a lawn mower has been tossed through it at 200 MPH.

Steel shutters and plywood are hauled out of storage sheds by prepared home owners and bolted over windows. Procrastinators will line up for hours at local home improvement stores fighting to get the last remnants of plywood so they can blast it over windows with 22 caliber nail guns at the last minute, making their house look like a drive by crime scene. As the storm draws nearer evacuation orders will be put in place by authorities and promptly ignored by residents. Battery operated radios, batteries, generators, bottles water, canned food, propane, grills, charcoal, candles, first aid supplies, baby food, and diapers will fly off store shelves so fast that the air rushing in to replace where they used to sit will form a giant whooshing sound. Fist fights at grocery stores, bulk food stores and mega stores will abound, and every single conversation in every single house hold, on every street corner, and in every coffee shop will be about nothing except the storm, how bad is it going to be, the latest wind speed, predicted landfall point and time, and current level.

In the aftermath of the storm personal attributes will be algebraically expanded in direct correlation to the proportion of the damage done by the storm. Descent people will be driven to do incredible feats of humanitarian good for their fellow human beings, and assholes will do horribly selfish and assholeish things to anyone that gets in their way.

One beautifully clear summer's day I was working the day shift as one of these fairly small cyclonic events churned its way across the Atlantic. At the time it was a considered a level three hurricane in a 1 to 5 system, and it was predicted to make landfall somewhere north of the airport later that night. Consequently, all through the day nonessential people that lived in this area were allowed to go home to prepare for the coming storm. Fortunately for me, I lived south and it looked like I was going to get to ride this one out.

As is usually the case with any weather event all of the things that needed to be in place to force the system to behave in the manner to which it had been predicted were not in place, and as the day wore on the predicted point of land fall moved ever farther southward, and toward my own home.   By three o'clock that afternoon when my shift was over, the thin red line on the map showing the projected path of the storm passed directly over my home. The storm was only about fifteen miles wide and small in comparison to other hurricanes but the ever increasing wind speed had elevated this storm to a level 4 with a sustained wind speed in excess of 130 MPH, and predictions were already being made that before it actually made land fall it would be a full blown level 5 hurricane with sustained winds in excess of 155 MPH. Additionally Hurricanes have a nasty habit of sucking the ocean level up higher than it normally is, this is called storm surge, and that is what causes most of the flooding. This storm had a predicted storm surge of 20 feet above normal. I did that math pretty quick, my house 6 feet above sea level + sea level increasing to 20 feet higher than normal = me trying to breath 14 feet under water.

I hadn't done a damned thing to get ready.

By the time I arrived home Mary had made the most of the time she had while I was at work watching the television in a wild eyed frenzy, and alternatingly praying to God that he not do anything bad to the house. Apparently God was busy driving his 155 MPH bulldozer at the east coast of the US and didn't hear anything Mary said.

My youngest stepson was in the Navy by this time and the two older kids were still living at home. I hurried to get them started moving all of the yard missiles into the garage. Since I no longer had a pool to throw anything into I had them stuff the lawn furniture into the garage as well. At least all of my wooden French doors would be easy to cover in wood. I started prying fence planks off the privacy fence that ran along the back yard, and I screwed these over the French doors.

"I sure hope that we're not doing this for no reason," Mary kibitzed over my shoulder.

'Yeah,' I thought 'I sure hope we get fucking pulverized so I didn't take down a fence and screw it into my doors for no reason.'

"Me too sweetheart," I said.

I was able to cover every door and window in the house except for a pair of larger glass sliding doors that sat at a right angles to each other on an inside corner of the back porch. I was just going to have to hope that nothing would be flying at the house from that direction. I filled both the bath tubs up with water because that's what I was told should be done to prepare for a hurricane, then I sent one of the kids to the gas station to fill all of our gas cans and cars with gas for the same reason. The idea of a 20 ft storm surge scared the hell out of me because the foundation of our house was only 6 feet above sea level. The only thing I could do to prepare for this was tie a rope off to one of the soil pipes sticking out of the roof so we could get up there in case the waters started to rise. The fact that we all would be climbing up that rope in the dark, fighting 155 MPH winds while water tried to drive us farther inland...or even the fact that there might not be any roof there at all when I needed one never occurred to me.

We finished all of our pre-natural disaster duties in the late afternoon and there was nothing left to do but wait. Mary and the kids stayed glued to the TV watching nonstop reports about how bad the storm would be and what to do to get ready. Naturally I stayed out of the TV room since the self-centered news networks still felt the need to hire female weather people and reporters. Buy this time in my journey through life with an abuser I knew better than to risk looking at another woman on television. I hadn't seen a movie, read a book, listened to the radio, read a newspaper or magazine, or watched television in nearly eight years. Each one of these Medias had been systematically shut down for me by Mary.

I made myself busy double, triple, and quadrupley checking, and rechecking all of the preparations we had made. Periodically someone would come out of the TV room and give me an update on storm strength, predicted landfall location, and time. Nothing was changing, and it was becoming more and more obvious that we were going to get our clocks cleaned sometime in the middle of the night.

Late that night everyone was in bed and I remember standing out in front of our house marveling at what a beautiful night it was. There was a warm gentle breeze blowing the palm trees around, and the street was deserted. The sky was a crystal clear deep black like highly polished ebony and the stars were dazzling. As I stood there by myself it was hard to believe that just a few miles to the east a horrible giant armed with winds that would exceed 200 MPH was moving steadily toward me carrying death and destruction that had not previously been seen in the United States. I wished we had evacuated, but Mary had made sure that we had been cut off from any form of family or friends so we had no place to go. I did the only thing left to do…I went back in the house and went to bed.

At about 1 AM I was jolted out of my sleep buy the howling wind of a large thunderstorm. I knew that this was just something that's called a feeder band that rolls out in front of a hurricane like a skirmish line in a civil war battle. Even though I knew that worst was yet to come, this storm was the strongest thunderstorm I had ever seen. As I looked out of the unprotected glass sliding doors, blinding flashes of lightning revealed trees bent over against the driving wind and rain. Water poured down from the sky in a constant relentless deluge…

…and then it stopped.

"Thank God" I thought. I knew that there was more to come but I was sure that wind had to have been close to hurricane strength, and we had weathered that portion of it. I woke Mary and the kids telling them that they had better take showers and get dressed. Mary ask what the hell was wrong with me, and I told her that I had no idea how long it was going to be before we were going to be able to have water again, the power was probably going to go out, and I didn't want everybody running around in the dark trying to find shoes and clothes in the event that we had to get outside and run around in debris. She grudgingly acquiesced.

As everyone placated me by getting ready for the rest of the storm I watched out the window, and the wind began to build again. It was now 2AM and the storm was going to start in earnest. While the visibility was still good I could see beautifully brilliant flashes of blue green on the horizon as electrical transformers blew up. The rain began to beat on the roof steadily, visibility dropped to a few feet, and the wind howled through the neighborhood like a beast prowling for victims. The wind picked up to the same point it had been at earlier and then surpassed it. Mary started begging to know what was going to happen next. I had nothing to tell her, so I just tried to reassure everyone that everything was going to be alright.

I was sure I was lying.

Soon the bagging on the roof and windward walls was constant as building materials that had recently adorned local yards as tool sheds and bird feeders slammed into the house like bullets.

With every noise Mary would wail, asking what that was. 'How the fuck should I know' was all that was screaming to get out of my mouth, but instead I tried to formulate some kind of intelligent answer. The lights flickered once then went out and we were plunged into total darkness. Soon there was a ripping sound coming from above us. I knew that parts of the roof were coming off, but I hoped that at least the plywood would stay on.

I looked out of the unprotected door again and every square inch of atmosphere was chocked with a grey mushy mess that sped past the window looking like someone had stirred up a giant glass of grey Metamucil. I knew that this grey crap was the blown in insulation coming from freshly opened attics all over the neighborhood. I also knew that we were screwed, it was only an hour into this thing, and I wasn't sure how much more the house could stand. That was about the time that water started pouring into the house through every light fixture in the ceiling. At least part of the roof was totally gone.

Mary was crying, and begging to know what was going to happen next, and the kids were holding their own. What was left of the roof was acting like a giant airfoil as the wind blew over it, and it was trying to lift the house off the ground, or detach itself. The vibration from this was shaking the house so bad that doors on cupboards in the kitchen flew open, and dishes crashed to the floor. Mary screamed, but the noise was so deafening that the only way I knew she was screaming at all was because I could see her mouth opened wide and the pained expression on her face.

Then, just like that, everything stopped. We all just looked at each other in wide eyed amazement. One of the kids and I forced one of the front doors open that was being wedged shut by all the trash that had blown against it. The sky was beautiful and full of stars just like it was earlier that evening before the storm. Flash light beams cut through the night all over the neighborhood reminiscent of the movie ET. Three giant Washingtonian Palms in my front yard had been laid down in a circle, and the house two doors down just wasn't there anymore. Clearly there had been tornados in the mix.

The part of the roof over the attached garage and kitchen of my house holding the rope ladder that was going to save us in the event of a flood was already gone, and there was debris everyplace. I looked up at the night sky to the east in wonderment that something that bad could have come and gone that quickly leaving that much damage in its path. That was when I saw the flash of repeated lightning strikes in the sky, revealing a giant wall of clouds and wind. We were standing in the eye, and the worst was yet to come.

I yelled at my stepson to get back in the house, and just as I slammed the door behind me the wind instantly picked up to the same levels that had just stopped a few moments before. It didn't take a slide rule to figure out that the house that had taken so much damage the first time around was at least in one piece when the wind started. This time it was already falling apart and we were about to get really clobbered with the dirty side of the storm.

The wind had switched around, and I could hear what was left of the roof leaving its current address in search of loftier climbs. Water was pouring in through the light fixtures even faster now, and the ceiling was beginning to bulge down under the weight of the water that was collecting in what once was the attic, and now was our only roof. The wind hammered directly into the exposed glass doors and I knew beyond any doubt that it was just a matter of time before one of the thousands of yard missiles trying to find a way through the glass was going to be successful.

"Everybody get into our closet!" I yelled at the top of my

lungs.

Everybody just looked at me. They couldn't hear a word I was saying. The air pressure was dropping so fast that my ears kept popping. I pointed the flashlight at my finger, and gestured at the master bedroom. Everybody started moving that way and I stood by the door to make sure that everyone got in OK. I moved to go through the door, and there was a giant crashing sound behind me as the tool shed from two doors down, complete with lawn mower and tools came crashing through the exposed glass doors and slammed into the wall next to me. I dove across the bed and herded everyone into our walk-in closet.

"What the hell was that?" one of the kids yelled.

I felt myself being sucked back out of the open closet door.

"I don't know," I screamed into his face "help me hold this closed!"

We both grabbed the center of the folding closet door, jerked it shut, and held it against the storm as it tried to pry it back open. We sat like that for the next hour and a half as the world was ripped apart just outside the stamped aluminum door.

The wind died down to a light 10 or 15 MPH, and hazy bits

of grey light started to show through the slats of the door we were still holding shut. The sun was starting to come up, and the realization that we had all lived through the storm was starting to spread across our collective consciousness.

I tried to push to door open but every ceiling in the house except the one in our closet had fallen in, and ironically it was trapping us in our safe house. We kicked the door through the wet dry wall and insulation and started to crawl out of our bomb shelter to see what was left of our house. The sight was stunning, and the farther I progressed through the mess the worse it got. Naturally, soaked drywall and insulation covered everything. In some places even that had been blown away revealing trash that had been blown in to the house right after the glass doors let loose. The shed, and all of its contents sat piled up in the corner of the living room and two thirds of the house sat totally exposed to the bright blue sky.

Right next to the glass door that had blown out sat the glass top to our dining room table. The wicker base and all four chairs were completely gone, never to be seen again, but the glass top rested on the wet carpet like someone had gently laid it there. Next to that sat a vase of silk flowers on a sofa table that hadn't even been touched. All of the living room furniture had been forced out through the double front doors and now sat in a perfect circle in the front yard. Of the three cars in the driveway, my truck was sitting on top of an electrical junction box by the street. My Chevette was upside down, and wrapped around a coconut palm, and Mary's Fiero, which had been sitting in between the two, was untouched. However the garage door had fallen in on her Corvette.

The white stucco front of our house had millions of tiny pieces of asphalt shingles embedded in it just like every other house in the neighborhood had, and everything was covered with a thin film of grey that had once been attic insulation. There wasn't a tree, fence, or mail box left standing as far as the eye could see, and pieces of house littered every square inch of yard.

"Why was our house hit worse than anyone else's?" Mary wined.

I looked over at the house that has no longer there, then at the air conditioner stuck in what was left of the roof across the street, then at the completely roofless house at the end of the street. I didn't know what Mary was looking at, but destruction look pretty much indiscriminate to me.

"I don't know sweetheart," I said absently.

All over the block the few people that hadn't left were coming out of destroyed homes to take assessment of what they had left. Everyone looked like they were in shock and walked around yards like they were in a dream. There wasn't so much as a piece of tar paper left on the little bit of roof that was still attached to the house. An air-conditioning compressor had punched a holed through one side of the plywood sheathing, traveled out the other side and was lying in the back yard next to a canoe. I figured that if this was the only shelter we were going to have I had better find a piece of plywood someplace and nail it over the hole.

I trudged off down the street to try and find a chunk of debris that would be big enough to cover the hole. Mary stayed in the front yard crying, and holding her dog. I found a fairly large piece of sheathing a few yards down the street and started dragging it home.

"What's that you're looting there mother fucker?" a familiar voice said from behind me.

I turned around to see one of the Hatfields standing in the front yard across the street from his own house. His giant gap toothed cousin stood next to him with a menacing grin on his face.

An even more menacing Mac-10 machine pistol dangled easily in his right hand.

"Blow me," I said as I kept dragging the junk to what was left of my house.

"Ya'll know we could shoot your ass for lootin'…right?" toothy said, twisting the Mac-10 around.

"I'm sure you'd fuck that up too," I said. The gun didn't mean anything to me. He would have been doing me a favor.

"What the hell's the matter with you…" my oldest step son yelled at the hillbillies. I saw him start to charge across the street at the hillbilly with the hand cannon.

"Don't!" I yelled as I ran to get between them.

BANG, BANG, BANG

Toothy fired the Mac into the ground about 2 inches from his own right foot. Thankfully that calmed everybody down and the Hatfields retreated into the house they were apparently guarding, laughing like children.

I went back to dragging my piece of wreckage over to my hovel so that I could try and throw together some type of makeshift shelter. It took a while to free a ladder from the debris that had piled up in the garage but persistence paid off, and soon I was sitting on top of what was left of my roof hammering a ripped up sheet of plywood over the hole.

The view from the roof was the most amazing thing that I have ever seen in my life. The only thing standing above ground level other than wrecked homes was the occasional Norfolk Pine trunk that had been swept clean of branches. Billboards, street signs, fences, everything else had been blown away. I could see forever with nothing to block my view, and as far as the eye could see was nothing but wreckage. I know that the analogy has been made many times since, but it looked just like a war zone. Bombed out houses everywhere and people in a state of shock walking around like zombies shifting through the rubble trying to salvage anything they could.

As I sat up there trying to figure out what my next move was going to be I heard the rotors of a helicopter beating up the air someplace behind me. When I turned around I saw one of the local news helicopters hovering over my house obviously filming the destruction, and even possibly filming the lone survivor sitting on his roof with a hammer and nails. Just like everyone else, I had seen these images before on television while I sat in the confines of my living room and clucked my teeth at the poor unfortunate refugee of some natural disaster. Now I was the guy everyone would be watching on TV as I tried to gather my life back together.

When I got back down off the roof Mary was totally despondent…which was actually a good thing. The only time that Mary seemed rational was when she was at her wits end. I would be able to deal with female desk clerks or cops or any other woman that we may need to deal with to take care of things, and Mary wasn't going to say anything. Naturally after things got back to normal she would always visit the fact that she was devastated that I actually had talked to a woman when we checked into a hotel, or asked a female cop if any roads were open to try and get out of the destruction zone, or whatever. But for right now I was actually going to be able to function. I would just have to take my lumps later.

"We have to get out of here," Mary said wide eyed "those lunatics across the street with a gun, and we don't even have a roof in case it rains."

I knew she was right. Everything in the house was soaked,

and most of the roof was gone. Both the front and back double doors were gone, and if the other gun shots we were hearing all over the place were any indication, looting was already well underway. It was time to gather our stuff and get the hell out of Dodge.

I cleaned as much crap as I could away from the Corvette on the inside of the garage and tried to gently pry the garage door off of it so as to not do more damage to it than was already done. The Fiero was in great shape so one of the kids could drive it. My stepson had a POS Sidekick that had the windshield ripped off of it, but other than that it was drivable. My S-10 pickup was going to be sitting on top of that junction box for a while keeping the inverted Chevette company, but at least we had three cars we could load whatever was left in and drive off.

The scene on the highway as we drove north was surreal. Cars that looked as though they had been flailed with a log chain ran windowless up and down the street dodging fallen trees, horizontal telephone poles, and parts of houses. Most of those cars had no glass at all left in them, and many of the drivers wore full face motorcycle helmets to their protect their heads from junk that was still blowing around the street. Occasionally a police car would drive by, windowless, and the lights on the roof smashed beyond recognition. The drivers were always in tactical gear, but it didn't matter. All communications towers had been destroyed and this was well before cell phones were common place. Anyone that needed emergency assistance…and that was most all of us…was on their own.

Mary was borderline catatonic until we got checked into the first hotel we found that had electricity. Fortunately that was only about 30 miles away. Once we got into the room she went hysterical. She was begging me to tell her that everything was going to be fine, and asking why God had done this to us, and accusing me of doing something to the house that made our damage worse than everyone else's. I was as busy as a cat covering up crap trying to stay ahead of her, and I was constantly losing ground.

I don't remember how or why, but the next morning I moved us into another hotel that was a little farther away but cheaper, and it actually had restaurants open near it. I had two more days before I was going to have to be back to work, so after I got everyone set up in the hotel room I went back to the house to start trying to get things cleaned up. There were very few people in the neighborhood, but the ones that were there all openly carried guns. The newspaper headlines the next day would read THE WILD WEST above a photo of a lone resident walking down a deserted street carrying a shot gun. I never worked down there unless I had a 25 automatic stuffed in my boot, and a 12 ga. at my side.

I stood in my front yard unable to even get an idea of where I was going to start. Then I saw a guy down the street drag some junk out of his front yard and drop it next to the street. That seemed like a good enough place to start for me so I started piling junk next to the place my mail box used to sit. It took me 2 days to make a dent in all of the junk just in the front yard of a ¼ acre lot, and the pile at the street was getting huge.

The next two weeks are mostly a blur now. I asked for and received two weeks of vacation time from work so I was able to try and bring what was left of the house back into some sort of semblance of order. Every day I would get up before the sunrise and drive down to ground zero. The looting, and general crime were way out of control so the National Guard had set up road blocks so they could restrict the flow of people in and out of the area. I had a federal job that required me to be able to move around, so I had a pass that allowed me to go anyplace I wanted. That would prove to be priceless in a month or so when the 82nd air borne showed up.

Once I got down there I would work in mind numbing heat until sunset, then drive back. It didn't take too long before the pile of trash grew so high on both sides of the street that you had to fling debris as high as you could just to get it on top of the pile. All of the streets in all of the neighbor hoods began to look like giant trash tunnels. The real fun started when people finally started taking the rotten food out of refrigerators that hadn't been running for two weeks. The stench was horrible and the rats and snakes were really starting to get out of hand. To this day when I smell rotting food in a garbage can or a land fill to takes me right back to hurricane days.

Eventually the U S Army Corps of Engineers had work crews going through all the neighborhoods with front end loaders and dump trucks clearing out all the trash. I remember that they made at least four runs...maybe more...but it was an incredible amount of debris. After I got the front yard cleaned I started on the inside of the house. As I said the fridge had to be cleaned out first. Then then tool shed decorating my living room, and all of its contents were added to Mt. Trashmore out front. After that all of the wet drywall from the ceiling and the insulation had to be drug out to the street followed by all the wet, by this time molding carpet and padding. Mary thought the kids were too traumatized to go back down to the house so I got to do all of this work alone.

I was in heaven!

Every one of the interior walls had been filled with water, so by the time I got to them they were all growing some kind of fungus, and little vine plants in them. So, out came every square inch of dry wall. Once that was all piled by the street I started cleaning out the garage, and the back yard. I was completely exhausted, and every night I would go back to the hotel and listen to Mary recount how my step son had saved our lives. How I was a worthless piece of shit, and without him we would all be dead, and how I had somehow totally screwed up our house so the storm could tear it apart worse than everyone else's. I didn't have the strength to even offer a comeback, and that generally made things worse.

Most of the insurance companies set up makeshift offices in a building near where Mary and I were staying. I called and asked if I could make an appointment to speak with ANY male claims adjuster. I had to get the living situation under control and Mary was just recuperated enough to screw us six ways to Sunday if I had to deal with a woman.

I went to the claims office and told them that if things continued the way they were I was easily going to go through the $18,000 temporary housing assistance that I was due according to my policy. I said that if they were to give me $10,000 dollars of that money right now I could buy a single wide mobile home to park in my front yard, and I wouldn't need the other $8,000. It was a win, win. Fortunately they saw it the same way I did, and within a few days there was a brand new single wide mobile home sitting up on concrete blocks on my front yard.

Now, every minute of every day could be consumed by one of three things; working at my job, working on my house, or fighting with Mary. Life was going to be swell. When I worked day shifts I worked on the house from the time I got home until I finally went to bed. When I worked night shifts I worked on the house from sunrise until I went to work. And on my days off...well I didn't get any days off.

Basically I was a zombie. Once I got to the rebuilding phase I decided to rebuild the house myself for several reasons. First I was concerned that I was either going to have to deal with contractors that I knew were going to end up banging Mary in the mobile home, which by this time I could have cared less about. I just knew that once they started rebuilding the house she was going to make it a total convoluted mess. Second, rebuilding everything myself would save us a ton of money, and more importantly occupy my time away from Mary's lunacy. Most of the time as I worked on the house Mary would be in the mobile home watching TV. The kids had jobs so they were gone a lot, and when they were home they watched TV with Mary, or went drinking with friends. Occasionally Mary would come into the house to inspect what I was doing, and inevitably a fight would start because a screw was crooked in a sheet of drywall or, the staples in some of the insulation weren't evenly spaced apart.

Once I got to the part where I was hanging full 4X8 foot sheets of drywall on the ceiling I made a makeshift H frame with 2X4 studs. That way I could slide one end of the dry wall sheet up on that while I screwed the other end into the ceiling. I'm 6'3" so I could almost reach the ceiling flatfooted, but standing on a bucket made things a lot easier. Unfortunately, continuously moving the buckets around for a better vantage point on the sheet I was working on was really eating up time. The fix I devised for that was to duct tape a bucket to each foot. That worked great…

Until Mary saw it.

I was in one of the back bedrooms sweating like a pig when I felt her standing behind me. I pulled a 2X4 up to hold the drywall sheet in place. I knew better than to wait until I finished what I was doing, no matter what it might be, before I acknowledged her presence.

"Hey," I said as I twisted around on my buckets to see her. She had her arms folded and was clearly not amused.

"What's the matter," I asked "did something happen."

"Are those buckets taped to your feet?" She asked blankly.

"Yep," I said innocently "pretty good idea right."

"You look like an idiot," she said

"Yeah, I know. But it really saves time."

"You know?" she said putting her hands on her hips. "You know that you look like a complete idiot, and you know that I might come in here at any time and see you like this, and you couldn't care less about how it might make me feel."

"But it really saves time," I said weekly. This wasn't the first fight that started like this since the storm. It happened so often that as I worked on the house I actually planned to have my work instantly interrupted for a few days while Mary expelled her grievances. That was why the 2X4 was leaning next to me in the first place.

"That's right," she said darkly as the colors started to flare on her mouth "it saves time for you, and you could care less that it makes me see you like a total fucking child that's just out here playing in the construction project."

"But sweetheart even professional drywallers use stilts on the job."

"That's right, stilts you shit head. They don't tape buckets on their feet. This is why I can't leave you out here alone. I have to check in on you all the time to make sure that you aren't doing anything stupid, or childish. I never know if you're going to try and start gluing those panels up, or think that it might be a good idea to fill the walls with dirt."

"That's a little farfetched don't you think."

"That's right you little pussy," she screamed "protect yourself!"

POW…she hit me in the nuts. I knew it was coming because that was how Mary always punctuated 'protect yourself'. It still hurt, but I just stood there.

She cocked back for another one and I caught her by the wrist.

She went totally nuts.

"Go ahead you abusive piece of shit," she screamed "Go ahead and manhandle me all you want you worthless fucker! I'm going to call the cops and have your ass dragged off to jail! All they have to see is the red mark on my wrist!"

She disappeared into the mobile home, and I followed right behind. I knew that that was exactly what she was going to do, and if I just followed her in the house and let her berate me as much as she wanted I wouldn't have to spend the night in jail being jacked with by cops that were going to "teach the wife abuser a lesson".

"Get the fuck away from me!" she creamed as I walked in the door.

"I'm sorry sweetheart," I said trying to calm things down.

"Yeah you're always sorry!" she said beginning to sob. "You pull whatever gay, childish, abusive shit you want, and then you think you can make it OK just by saying you're sorry."

"I know…" the next words out of my mouth were going to be 'I'm sorry' and I caught them just in time.

"Without me you'd be nothing," she went on "you wouldn't be able to do anything with this house, you wouldn't be anything at your job, and you'd just be blowing guys in the parking lot of some gay bar for money."

"I'm trying…"

"You always are trying. Trying this, and trying that! When the hell are you going to stop trying and start doing? When the hell do I get to start having what all the other women in the world get to have from their husbands? Do you think that any of the other women in this neighborhood are having this stupid fucking conversation with their husbands right now?"

I could feel that I was beginning to get pissed off and that was never a good thing. "I don't see any of the other husbands in this neighborhood busting their asses all night, and day just so their wives can have some extra money." I said matter-of-factly.

SLAP! She hit me in the face.

"I'm sorry," I said. Instantly back in control again and

making like the assault never happened. "I know how hard all of this is on you and I'm spending most of my time out in the house."

"You don't know anything," she said "It's because of bullshit like this that I have to go to other men. What do you think I'm doing while you're at work? I have to go out and find someone that's going to make me feel like a woman."

I didn't say anything. I had heard all of this a million times before. I knew that she was banging her way through most of the clientele at the bar where she found her first distraction and I couldn't have cared less. If that kept her busy, and off my back then that was great.

"I'll be done with this house as soon as I can be," I said "then we can get things back to normal."

I knew that those words were a mistake as soon as they came out of my mouth. It was like lighting a cannon fuse then jumping in front of it to listen to the boom.

"BACK TO NORMAL! What the hell is normal for you? I've had to carry you and be your mommy ever since the first day I met you. Is that normal to you? A normal man would want things to be better. A real husband would be telling his wife that things were

243

going to be better. Not you though. Oh hell no, as long as you can keep me right where you want me you're just as happy as a kid in a candy store."

Everything after that was just more, and more of the same old thing, hour after hour of accusations, a punch to the balls here, and a slap to the face there. At one point after the sun came back up Mary was standing at the sink cutting something up and she swung the knife at me again. It took it out of her hand like it was a common everyday occurrence. Once she ran out of steam I went back to work, and she went to bed.

Trips to the local building supply store were a real blast as well. Naturally Mary had to come with me because she couldn't trust me to go there alone, and not try to pick women up. When I went there I was always buying a lot of building materials that were going to have to be delivered. I had to spend quite a bit of time with the sales guy there making sure that they had the list of what I needed right, and working out a delivery date.

One day Mary came over to me while the guy I was working with was on the phone. She had been out in the garden department or something looking around while I was busy.

"One of the guys that work here paid me a compliment," she said coyly.

"I'm not surprised," I said "what did he say?"

"He said 'excuse me, I know that I've never seen you before, and I could probably get into real trouble for this, but why is such a nice, and beautiful woman like you married to such an asshole'?"

"Who said that to you?" I really didn't care who said it, or even that they had said anything to her at all. I knew that it hadn't happened in the first place. I mean what kind of a pickup line was that anyway? *Excuse me miss but I'm going to put my job in jeopardy by calling your husband an asshole in the hopes that this will allow me entry into your petticoats.* I simply knew what was expected out of me in the way of feigned indigence and I was playing the part. I demanded to know who this guy was. Mary continued to refuse to tell me because I was just going to embarrass her.

Eventually it was obvious that Mary had gotten all of the attention that she wanted, and was ready to go home. I made one last perfunctory demand to know who this cad was, she was happy and we left.

245

By this time I was running on pure momentum. Someone could have dropped a dead body on my head and I simply would have shrugged it off and kept working. Interestingly, no one around me seemed to notice. I guess as long as the pay check kept coming in the condition of the provider of that check was irrelevant.

TWENTY FIVE;

I came home one night after a night shift, and there was no Mary in the house. All I wanted to do was go to bed, but I knew that I was expected to go out and find her. Otherwise what would turn into a few hours of lost sleep while I went hunting for her would turn into another marathon fight. Finding her wasn't all that hard. I went straight to the bar.

When I went inside I saw Mary sitting at the bar talking to some guy. I was less than surprised.

I walked over and stood between them. "Hey," I said to Mary, ignoring the latest conquest.

"Hey," Mary said moodily, clearly wishing that I would get lost and leave her to her pastime.

"I'm Jim," the idiot that was trying to pick up my wife said as he thrust his hand toward me.

I shook his hand and introduced myself.

"He's a pilot too." Mary said indicating the life support system for a penis that was standing next to me.

"Really," I said "what do you fly?"

247

"I'm flying a Citabria right now," he said with a smile that would have fit better on a six year old boy in a school yard "but what I'm really into is helicopters. Do you like helicopters?"

"Yeah I do as a matter of fact," I answered him as I looked at Mary.

"No, I don't just mean like them," he said over enthusiastically "I mean do they actually give you a real live hard on. Not just as a matter of speaking. I mean does the thought of a helicopter actually make your dick hard."

"No Jim, I can't say that a helicopter ever actually made my dick hard."

"Look," he said "I have to go take a piss, don't go away, I'll be right back."

Mary looked like she wanted to shoot me.

"What's the matter," I asked. It seemed like a legitimate question since all I had done was show up and thwart the opening innings of an away game of hide the wiener.

"I was just having a bad night, and I felt like coming here," she said.

"Did something happen at home?"

248

"No."

"Do you want me to stay with you?"

"No I just want to be alone."

"OK, I'll go home. Call me if you need anything."

Mary just looked at the floor.

I left.

What happened next at the bar was obvious. Jim cane back out, he and Mary talked for a little while, He took her back to his place, and according to the blow by blow details that Mary provided me with after the fact, they tried out every page of the Kama sutra until Mary could barely walk right.

After I got home I paced up and down the street until 2 or 3 in the morning. Eventually Mary pulled into the driveway looking like she had been drug through a knot hole backwards. I asked where she had been, and she instantly told me that she had gone home with Jim, then she had driven around for a while so her hair could dry out.

Just like all of the times before, I wasn't mad, glad, hurt, happy, or anything in between. I was just numb to what my life had become. I've put a lot of thought into that night over the course of the last several years. Not because I love to relive things like that, but instead because I feel that if a person has no inward reflection then you can never really understand yourself let alone the human condition.

I remember that right after I ran away and hid from Mary I reestablished contact with my parents, and I was sitting on their back porch relaying the very story that I just told above. My mother was horrified, and I honestly had no idea why. It reminded me of a letter I had sent home as a teenager in the Navy. We had been out to sea in the Mediterranean for 8 months, and had just finished 30 consecutive days on line providing air support over Lebanon while Americans were evacuated from the city during the civil war there.

In this letter home to my parents I had made more than one reference to the "fucking Navy" and the "fucking assholes" that I served with. I never even thought about it. This was the only thing that I had been around for the past 8 months and I had become so used to it that it was just common parlance for me. Needless to say I received a very stern letter from my father, and that was all it took to snap me back into reality.

In the early days of my resurrection as a human being, after I extricated myself from the mess my life had become, I convinced myself the reason I handled Mary's infidelity the way I did was because I didn't love her anymore, and if she was banging someone else then at least she wasn't expecting anything from me. Even when I used to actually say that out loud it seemed hallow to me. I even asked myself if I didn't say those things to protect my current wife from the pornographic past that I had lived with Mary, and I think that that was possibly the case. Because when I strip the entire sorted situation bare of all pretense and physiological armor plating I realize that I was far from indifferent to Mary's extramarital activities.

In fact I had become deeply complicit. Once I came to that realization I had to try and analyze why I would ever do something like that. I knew that there was such a thing as an "open" marriage, but I also knew that that wasn't what this was. I wasn't sexually excited about Mary's sexual habits, and the last thing that *I* wanted was to have any type of affair. Mentally I had been conditioned to think only about what Mary wanted, and about what would make Mary happy. I know now that if Mary had asked me to go out and find men for her I would have gladly done that.

Mary had always dangled in front of me the possibility that things in our marriage could be ok if I would just fix this one last thing, and now sex with other men was just one more step in that ladder. By this time Mary loved to tell me what other men had done to her while she and I were having sex. It was clearly exhilarating to her to tell me how experienced they were, or how much better, or larger than me they were. She talked about how many times they made her cum, or positions they forced her into. She clearly loved that, and the only feeling I had was that at least I was doing something that made her happy.

Nothing that I'm telling you here is an excuse or justification for the things that I did or the things I condoned. I'm simply saying that I was conditioned to except, and function in the reality that I was given. It took a long time for me to understand the things that I've just written, and even to this day I look back on those things and I'm disgusted by the things that I allowed myself to become.

TWENTY SIX:

Things were progressing with the house. I had hauled 30 rafters up on the lentil by myself, set them, tied them down with hurricane straps, and braced the gable ends. The 4X8 foot sheets of roof sheathing were delivered, so I hauled them up a ladder one at a time, shimmed them and nailed them in place. After that I hauled all of the 30 paper up, all the roofing nails, and tin tabs, and nailed that in place. Next came the bundles of shingles. One at a time up the ladder they went, and were stacked on the peak of the roof, and installed.

After I was done with the roof, and interior work I hired a company to install the carpet and we were ready to move back into the house. A lot of things still needed to be done inside like painting, base boards, and molding, some doors and cabinets needed to be hung. But at least we could move out of the mobile home in the front yard so that I could start working on the outside of the house.

I placed an ad in the paper selling the mobile home for next to nothing, and in no time some mobile home park came and moved the monster off what was left of the lawn. Both of the step kids had moved into a rented trailer in a park south of where we lived so it was just Mary and I in the house now, but the change was mostly transparent. The fighting still continued constantly, and Mary still dabbled in her past time of sport fucking with strangers.

Now that I was mostly working outside in the yard Mary was becoming increasingly unhinged about the other women that lived on the neighborhood. She told me that if the woman across the street was out working in her yard she didn't want me working anywhere where the neighbor could see me. Mary said that she knew that this woman would try something with me just to get even with her (for what I don't know) and that I would be too stupid or too much of a pussy to stop her.

One day I was working on a deck on the side of the house that was connected to French doors that opened into the television room. Mary walked out onto the deck and she was livid. Apparently the woman across the street had been cutting the grass in her front yard the entire time I had been working on the deck. I hadn't even noticed, but Mary had been sitting in the house the entire time watching the clock, and steaming because I hadn't dropped what I was doing to come in the house until she was gone.

That fight lasted for about 2 days. I remember that there was a lot of screaming, and accusations tossed around that I was in fact having an affair with the neighbor. Why else would I openly defy Mary like that, and rub her nose in the fact that we were "making eyes" at each other across the street. At some point all of my clothes were tossed out in the front yard, and I spent the night in the parking lot of the gas station down the street.

Every day it was something new, and it was impossible to keep up with all of the things that Mary was accusing me of doing. One day I walked out of the back door to start working on the privacy fence around our backyard. I was still putting my belt on as I walked out and Mary went nuts. She said that she was stupid enough to want to think that she was the only one to ever see me getting dressed, and that even though I couldn't even give her that, the least I could do was not force her to watch me get dressed in front of every other woman in the community.

Another marathon fight...more punches to the nether regions...more slaps to the face more nights in the parking lot of the local gas station. By this time Mary had demanded that I not touch her anymore. According to her nothing else had forced me to grow up, so maybe if she completely cut me off from even the slightest physical contact I would have to start acting the way that she wanted me to. In retrospect this was also about the same time that Mary had told me out of the blue that if I allowed her to have an affair with her daughter's boyfriend she would never forgive me for it. It's obvious to me now that they were already banging away at each other. The edict that I wasn't too touch her was born out of some sort of adolescent loyalty to her new side bar, and the fact that I was supposed to keep her from doing it was just making sure that she had someone to heap the blame on when they got caught.

Since it was now just the two of us in the house Mary was becoming increasingly paranoid about someone breaking into the house and raping her. The obvious fact that all anyone needed to do was ring the doorbell, and they would be blown within minutes was lost on her. Mary talked me into keeping a loaded shotgun in the bedroom next to the doors that led out to our new pool deck. I was pretty sure that the only person this shotgun was going to be used on was me, but the fact that it was there seemed to keep Mary happy about her security.

One day I had been laying ceramic tile on part of the concrete deck behind the infamous glass sliding doors since sun up. I had an afternoon shift that day so I wanted to get as much done as I could in the morning. I had gotten in the habit of making Mary's coffee every morning and setting it on her bedside table in an insulated container along with the newspaper so it would be there when she got up. There had been a previous terrible fight about this, because if I cared about her at all I would have realized that the paper left ink smudges on our white quilt when she read it in bed, so I should stop doing it.

After I stopped leaving the paper we had another fight because I should have found a way around the problem of the ink smudges. Obviously I didn't care about her in the first place and to her the only reason I ever started leaving coffee, and the paper in the first place was to make me look like a big deal. She was sure that I told all of my girlfriends at work, and around the neighborhood that I was the greatest guy in the world for taking care of my wife like that. She certainly didn't want anything done for her that was only being done to make me look better. Eventually a compromise was reached and I would leave the coffee and the remote for the TV at her bedside. Then I would leave the newspaper in the TV room so she could read it after she got up.

As I worked on the deck I heard Mary up and moving around in the house so I went in to tell her how the project was coming. I walked into the master bath where Mary was putting on her makeup. When I saw the reflection of her face in the mirror I instantly knew I was in the very deepest of shit.

"What's the matter sweetheart?" I asked.

"I really don't need any of your stupid bullshit today," she said to me as she slid lipstick over her lower lip accentuating the lovely blue green hue on her chin.

"How could I have done anything already? I haven't even talked to you yet." I was at a complete loss.

Mary walked out of the bathroom, and opened the door to the walk in closet next to our bed...and that's when I saw it.

Sitting on the night stand next to Mary's side of the bed was a black and chrome stylish thermos of coffee, a coffee mug, and the daily paper.

I was certain that if I went out to the TV room I would see the remote for the bedroom TV sitting where the newspaper should have been. In my early morning stupor I had put the wrong things in the wrong place, and I was about to pay for it.

(As I sit here preparing to write this next part I'm completely conflicted. I'm asking myself why I let things get this far out of control. I'm asking myself why I wasn't strong enough to put a stop to the insanity, why I didn't just clock the shit out of Mary. I know that I had every right too, but I also knew that mentally I simply couldn't. It would have been no different than if she had physically tied my arms behind my back, and used me as a punching bag.

My current dilemma stems from the fact that if I feel like a spineless, poor excuse for a man right now, how can I expect anyone else to feel otherwise? For almost a week I've put writing off because I'm starting to feel that I have simply compiled 170 some odd pages of proof that I really am a worthless piece of shit. Maybe that's exactly what I have done...maybe not.

I really don't know anymore.

I don't even know if I'm going to help anyone with this work. Maybe all I'll do is more damage.

Who knows?)

I don't feel the need to go into all of the "Fuck you," "No...fuck you," dialog here because it's the same as every other ignorant screaming match that I have documented here in this telling of my tale. Mary ranted on hour after hour compiling her list of grievances that I had done nothing to fix. I defended myself verbally. Insults, and accusations were spit around the room in mini-gun like speed, with the same deadly affect, and eventually the hitting started.

Mary cocked back to let me have a good hot shot in the face and I grabbed her wrist.

"Stop fucking hitting me," I said in a threatening tone that surprised even me.

Mary stopped dead in her tracks and the oddest look that I have ever seen in my life veiled down over her face. To this day I can't describe it. We stood there for what seemed to me like an eternity looking in to each other's eyes. I, with my look of resigned indifference to whatever happened next, and Mary with the stoic look of a serial killer.

She jerked her arm free of my grasp, and walked swiftly into the bedroom. I was standing there trying to decide what point in our dance of ignorant desperation we were currently in. Where we at the part where the drinking started? Where we at the point where my clothes were about to take one more unceremonious trip out into the front yard followed by my own sorry ass, on the way to spending the night in my car in the parking lot of a gas station? Or was this the part where Mary locked herself in the bed room, and faked phone calls to either my parents or my place of employment.

Instantly my questions were answered when Mary came quickly out of the bedroom carrying the shot gun slung low at her side like a confederate infantry man charging the Union lines at the stone wall in Gettysburg. All I had time to think was *"What the fu..."* before the business end of the 12 gauge rammed into my stomach so hard that it nearly knocked me over.

Mary pulled the trigger...

The room was filled with the deafening click of a firing pin falling on a recently emptied chamber. I had taken the shell out of the gun just days before because I could see Mary blowing someone away by accident in the middle of the night.

Mary looked down at the gun with the quizzical look that someone might give a TV remote that refuses to turn the set on. The only thing she didn't do was shake it and pull the trigger again.

While she was trying to figure why her shot gun wasn't working I gently reached down, pulled it away from my stomach and out of her grasp. I propped it in the corner.

"Look at you," Mary said disgustedly "you don't even care what it makes me feel like when you make me do something like that."

And just like that we were right back in the fight. It was like the serious murder attempt had never even happened. I had no idea what Mary was thinking but I was seriously thinking that I had two options. Either try to get the hell out, or make sure that I always kept the shot gun loaded. I really had no idea which one I wanted to do.

TWENTYSEVEN:

As hard as it is to believe, things between Mary and I really started to go downhill after the shot gun incident. She was spending more time at the bar, and from the stories that she told me later she was having a penis sampling contest out there that would rival any Dodge City hooker. Oddly enough the more that Mary banged her way through her favorite haunt, the more jealous she became of me. Fight after fight erupted because I would be caught in or near the front yard while some woman, someplace on our street was in view of our house. Sometimes Mary would call me into the TV room and show me some cheap ring that she was interested in on QVC or HSN and ask me what I thought of it.

She caught me off guard the first time she did this because I had no idea that this was a test to see if I would acknowledge the model that was showing off the jewelry. When I told her what I thought of the ring, and made no mention of the model we were instantly off to the races. Clearly I was impressed with the woman on TV because I didn't say anything about her. If I had cared about our relationship I would have acknowledged the model, and put Mary's mind at ease about it.

The next time I was set up I acknowledged the model, and we were off to the races again because I loved to rub her nose in the fact that I couldn't keep my eyes off of other women. Of course she knew that the real problem was the fact that I was gay, and I was using women to over compensate for the fact that I real needed a penis in my mouth. I had no problem with being gay, or not being gay, any more than I had a problem with loving other women. Those thought simply didn't exist, and there was no way to convince Mary of that.

During this time Mary was a veritable flesh magnet according to her. Guys were hitting on her every place. They were trying to get her to come home with them at the gym. They were trying to pick her up at the grocery store. One day she went to the beach, and some guy spent the entire day talking to her. When they left he walked her to her car, pushed her up against it, and started kissing her. He even went so far as to start to pull her bathing suit bottoms down and screw her right up against the car in public. She stopped him, but made it clear to me that it wasn't because she didn't want it, but instead because she didn't want to get arrested for public indecency.

Sometimes delivery men in the shopping market would try and pick Mary up. Apparently they would try to work their magic on her by giving her free food. After an incident like this Mary would ask me how I liked something that I was eating. If I said I did she would tell me, with a sly little grin that so and so that was trying very hard to get in her pants, and given it to her. At first I was indifferent to this. Anyone that wanted her could have her. Besides, it was painfully obvious that the majority of these stories were pure bullshit designed to make me jealous. Consequently, if I failed to get cranked up about them we would be in another knock down drag out fight.

One day while Mary and I were on our way to the local home improvement store Mary mentioned that she had "won" a three day cruise to the Bahamas. My first thought was that there was absolutely no way that I was going to go on a cruise ship to the Bahamas with Mary. Obviously there would be women every place, usually in bathing suits, and we would be in one long perpetual fight. While I was contemplating how I was going to get out of this one Mary told me that she was thinking about going with her daughter.

"I think that's a great idea," I said like an idiot who had no idea he was walking right into a well thought out trap. "I still have a lot of work to do on the house and it might be a good break for you guys to go do that together."

"So that would be OK with you," Mary asked without the slightest indication in her voice that she might have a problem with it.

"Sure," I said "you guys would have a great time, and I could have the house nearly done when you got back."

"That's true," Mary said looking out of the window indifferently. "And with your female problem a cruise might not be the best thing for us to do."

And now the moment of truth. Mary sat in her seat deceptively serene like a picador waiting for her *tercio de varas.* All I needed to do was offer her the back of my neck. If I agreed then we were off to the races because the fact that I knew it, and did nothing to fix it made me an insensitive careless piece of shit. If I denied it then I was all of the above, but in this case it was because I didn't care enough about her to confront the hell that I put her through.

Since the outcome had clearly been decided, I chose option A. If nothing else that would ensure that there was no way I was getting on a cruise ship with Mary.

"I know sweetheart," I said "and I'm sorry, but you guys would have a great time together."

Of course the battle was instantly on. Insults and accusations were thrust by the attacker and parried by the defender. Every time reason was interjected into the fray it was unceremoniously stomped to death, eaten, and regurgitated into the street. Back and forth we went with no clear strategy, and no kind of a withdrawal plan. We were simply locked in mortal everlasting combat like the half black, half white faced aliens on the original Star Trek series. Wrongs committed by me from seven, eight, even nine years before were broken over my head and stuffed down my throat.

I certainly didn't want to take this insane melee into anywhere public, so Mary and I just drove around town for a little while taking our vaudeville act of hate and discontent up and down the highway. Eventually I turned for home with Mary still screaming in my ear, I pulled up in the driveway, and left the car running.

"I don't want to take this into the house," I said. At least in the moving car she would hesitate to try and kill me out of self-preservation if nothing else. "Just ride with me, and we can work this out."

Mary refused at first but I persisted, and eventually she grudgingly acquiesced. As soon as we left the driveway I knew that I had totally screwed up. I should have just gone into the house and taken whatever lumps I was going to get. As I drove down the street it occurred to me that I had nothing to say that was going to make any of this better. I hadn't come up with anything new to say from the start to finish of this fight, and for that matter I hadn't been able to come up with anything to make things less crazy since the day I met her. I had no idea why I thought it was a good idea to promise Mary a good outcome if she just came with me in the first place, because I knew that it was never going to happen.

These were the thoughts that were meandering through my head when I heard Mary vocalize her thoughts.

"You fucking worthless piece of shit!" Mary screamed. That part wasn't a surprise to me, but when she punctuated her distain by grabbing two fists full of my hair, and start slamming my head into the left side window of the car she had my attention.

Mary had one knee up in her seat and was ramming my head into the window has hard as she could. I guess the only thing that kept it from breaking was the fact that I kept resisting as much as my neck would allow as I tried to maintain control of the car. Eventually I jerked my head forward to try to get myself free of her wild eyed grasp, and that worked. Albeit at the expense of slamming my own forehead into the steering wheel from the inertia of Mary losing her grasp.

I felt pretty light headed, and I was trying to stay with it so I didn't kill an innocent passerby when I lost consciousness and drove up on the sidewalk. Then *thwack,* Mary caught me right in the throat with the heal of her left hand. That just about finished the job when it cut of my air so I pulled over to the side of the road and stopped. I don't remember what was said at that point, and to be honest I don't even remember driving home. All I remember is walking back into the house with Mary right behind me saying something about if I cared for her at all I wouldn't make her do things like that to me, or call me names.

Once in the house my head started to clear, and we were right back into it again. The sun was starting to go down, and I watched as dusk turned to dark, and the street lights came on casting muted shadows sporadically around the house. As a child I loved the beauty of this time of day. I have grown to detest it now. Eventually the stars gave way to dusty pinks and blues of a new sunrise. I called in sick for work, Mary stomped around the house lamenting ever having met me, and rehashing the rehashed hash that had become my life. The sun rose dutifully over the house, and retreated from one more day of hatred, leaving only dark and soft light of the street lamps once again.

Mary and I were facing each other, both bathed in the greenish glow of artificial halogen light, and swimming in a sea of self-pity, and loathing. I was alternating between trying to keep my focus due to lack of sleep or food, and trying to say whatever would put an end to this insanity.

Mary said something and I missed it.

"What?" I said.

WHAM! Her left fist caught me by surprise and connected with the right side of my face. I had promise Mary long ago that I would never put her through my going to a dentist or a doctor, because she could never live with having to watch me allow another woman to touch me. When the irresistible force of her fist met the unyielding mass of my face I instantly felt two badly neglected teeth gratefully snap off at the root and lay in a bloody pool on my tongue.

There was no question in my mind that if Mary knew she had just knocked my teeth out there was going to be hell to pay. We had been going at this for two days now, and if I was "insensitive" enough to show her that I had "forced" her to do that to me things were going to get much worse.

I swallowed them.

At some point before the sun came up the fight ended. I don't remember if Mary ran out of steam or just gave up, but I know I swallowed quite a bit of blood before the brand knew holes in my mouth finally clotted over. Later I was treated to one of the most poignant metaphors I've ever seen or heard of. I was standing in the bathroom after an odd feeling bowel movement, and there, before me, in the toilet were both of my teeth resting comfortably in my own excrement. The gravity of the scene was far from lost on me, because for over a decade I had been forced to eat shit to survive, and now I was looking the literal translation of my very existence.

I had never wished harder for a full blown heart attack to blissfully carry me out of existence than I did at that very moment.

But I wasn't to be that lucky. Life went on, and on, and on, one miserable day after another. I was simply a meat puppet dancing on strings that were held in place by Mary. If there was a birthday or holiday or family get together I would display the happy me that everyone expected to see. Holidays, and Mary's birthday were particularly hard to deal with because I was expected to preform like any other husband and shower her with gifts and thoughtfulness. But in the perpetual catch 22 that I lived in, Mary would go nuts if I went to the mall without her, so I could surprise her with a gift. This was before the days of internet shopping. If I didn't get her anything I was even in deeper trouble. If I tried to talk to her about it, then I was a child that had to have his wife explain to him how she should be treated. To this day I hate holidays and birthdays with the white hot intensity of a thousand suns.

If I wasn't working on the house I was working at work. If I wasn't doing either of those things I was cutting the grass, washing the cars, or sweating to death in a hot garage with the door down as I peeked out of the windows waiting for some housewife or another to go back inside so I could continue what I was doing in the yard.

When I wasn't doing any of these things I was fighting with Mary, and since the shot gun incident I never went to bed before she did, and I never stayed in bed after she got up. I was in flat out survival mode, and what little shred of self that I had to cling onto was gently slipping out of my grasp, and before too long I would fall hopelessly into the abyss of insanity that Mary called home.

TWENTYEIGHT:

I viewed my job as sanctity. The only Mary induced stress there was crapping my pants every time the outside phone rang, and worrying either who was going to answer it, or if there was going to be a females voice that could be over heard in the background should the caller be Mary. I pretty much had all the women I worked with hating the very sight of me so, as I said before I wouldn't have to worry about a chance meeting in public.

I spent any break time that I had working on training videos for the facility. I had quite a few years in at my job, we had a lot of new people, and I felt that I could do some good helping people be better at what we did. The training videos led to teaching the occasional class during our team training sessions once every two weeks. My male fellow co-workers would have a good time ribbing me during these classes, and my female co-workers busied themselves glairing holes in my forehead.

One day I was giving a class on a piece of technical equipment that we all used, but no one really knew how it worked. I had one of these things all torn apart on a desk top, and I was teaching one of the teams how to use it correctly. Sitting in the class room was one of the most beautiful women that I had ever seen in my life. She was stunning in that unassuming "I have no idea how good I look" kind of way. Tall, slender, blond hair, and blue grey green eyes that could look right into your sole, and leave you thinking about her long after you had been first infected by her smile.

I knew right off that I was going to have to shit on this one extra hard.

But she just kept sitting there…smiling at me!

I remember thinking 'Hey dumb ass, don't you know who I am?' So before class started I shot a steely glare her way.

"HI Dave," she said sweetly, instantly melting my feigned assholeishness.

"Hi," I mumbled. 'Jesus Christ!' I thought 'what the hell is the matter with you? You just talked to…*one of them.*'

In over 11 years of living in the hell that I have documented above I had only ever related anything of my home life to two people. One was Kenny Durham, and the other was Larry Summers. These two people were true friends, and never once questioned me or my methods. Although they only knew a small part of what I was going through the conversations I had with them were about the only thing that kept me from ventilating my own head.

After the infamous training room incident I went to Larry and asked him about the blond in class that day. I already knew her name was Christy but I didn't know what her situation was. The fact that I was even verbalizing interest in a female scared the living shit out of me. But I had apparently lost control of my own faculties. Larry beat that control right back over my head.

"She's engaged," he said flatly.

So that was that then. But to my own shocked amazement I couldn't let go. Christy and I became friends. I had no earthly idea how to handle that, and it was a very darkly dangerous thing to have happen to me. When I talked to her I felt things that I hadn't felt in a very, very long time. I started to look forward to something. I couldn't wait to get to work now just so I could see her. I knew that this was never going to go anyplace, but I could do nothing more to stop what I felt than I could wish the tide to stop rising.

I was always careful not to touch her because I knew just as surely as I knew the sun was going to come up the next morning as soon as I touched Christy all of my plutonic control was going to go speeding out the window with a haste that would make Chuck Yeager's breaking of the sound barrier look like a Sunday stroll in the park. We talked about work, and life in general. I never mentioned my home life, and purposefully kept her fiancé out of the conversation. I learned that we had the same love for Jimmy Buffet music; she hated the Beatles because their music was sappy, she had been a Hendrix freak since the age of 10, she loved basketball, practical jokes, and she had a wicked sense of humor.

I knew that I was falling deeply in love with her, and I knew that there was nothing I could do about it, but it was like a life raft to a drowning man. It was also the most dangerous thing that I had ever allowed myself to do to that point in my life. I found an old

Jimmy Buffet cassette someplace, and I would listen to '*A pirate looks at forty*' and '*Son of a sailor*' over and over again as I drove home from work. Before I pulled into the driveway I would hide the tape under the carpet behind the seat of my truck like a WWII Stalag prisoner hiding escape tools.

All I could think about was Christy. It welled up inside of me, and consumed every waking moment that I had. It was just a matter of time before all of that emotion spilled out onto Mary's floor, and was going to have to be cleaned up. She and I were eating dinner one night after Christy and I had had a conversation at work about playing practical jokes.

"What would you do if I were to hold the trigger down on the spray nozzle at the kitchen sink with a rubber band, and you got wet when you turned on the water," I asked innocently.

Inside my head there was a little man running around waving his arms yelling "Stop, stop you idiot! Turn back! Danger Will Robinson, danger!" But on the outside I just sat there with a stoic, if not serene look on my face waiting for the answer.

"Why would you do that?" Mary asked with the exact same peaceful look she had on her face the day she ambushed me with the Bahamas cruise.

"Because I think it would be funny," I said

"You, and your fucked up sense of humor has gotten us to the place that we're in right now, and you would do that because you think it's funny," she was on a slow, downhill roll to crazy town, and picking up steam. The fact that I really didn't care scared me a little.

"Explain how abusing your wife like that is funny to you," she went on "would you think it was funny to knock me down in the front yard? What's next? Would you think it was funny to tie me to the bumper of your truck, and drag me through the mud?"

"No," I said "I don't think…"

"That's exactly right, you don't think," she glared at me "you don't ever think. You just do what eve the hell you want, and never think about how it's going to affect me."

"That's not what I'm saying. I…"

"If either of my boys ever treated their wives like that I'd never talk to them again. I'd tell them that I was done with them until they decided to grow up, and act like adults."

That fight lasted at least into the night, I don't remember anymore because they were all starting to melt into each other, and one violent act was beginning to look like all of the violent acts before it. I remember at some point Mary used my scrotum for a punching bag again, and I got slapped a few times, but I really couldn't have cared less because I knew that I would get to see Christy the next day.

A few days after that event I was talking to Larry about Christy.

"When are you going to quit dicking around and do something about that?" he asked me.

"What can I do," I said "she's engaged to some guy, and this is never going to go any farther than it already has. Hell, it's already gone too far."

"She's not engaged anymore," He said smiling.

"What?" I asked. I couldn't believe what he was saying. I felt as though I might drown in a vast sea of emotion that was washing over me.

"I said, she's not engaged any more. I assumed you knew that already."

"Why the hell would you assume that?" I said in disbelief "We never talk about him."

"Yeah," he said "I know."

"How long have they been broken up?" I asked.

"She broke things off shortly after she said hello to you in that idiotic training class you were giving."

"Why the hell didn't she say anything to me?"

"Because you're married dip shit. She knows there will never be anything between you two."

I stood there staring at him blankly. I didn't even know how to feel about the world I lived in now. I felt light headed, and I was sure that the floor beneath me was going to swallow me up into infinite darkness, and never release me. I had to act, but what was I going to do? I had a mess to clean up that was uncleanable, and I knew that someone like Christy was not going to be unspoken for very long.

"You know," Larry said "watching you two dinks dance around each other is almost painful."

TWENTYNINE:

On Sunday mornings in the place where we worked, it was fairly common practice for a few co-workers to sneak out for breakfast before things started to get too busy. I had formulated a plan in my head, and I was ready to put it into action. This was a very delicate matter, and it had to be handled like that. One wrong move and my only hope of salvation in life would slip through my grasp, and leave me with nothing. I knew exactly what was at stake. Behind door number one was the rest of my life in happiness, and behind door number two was an eventual loaded gun, and a giant, almost comical exit hole in the back of my head. My longevity on the face of this planet would rest on whatever I did next.

"Would you like to get some breakfast?" I asked Christy.

"Sure," she said.

"Where would you like to go," I asked knowing that it didn't make any difference.

"Anyplace is fine, I'll go get my purse, and let them know we're leaving," she said.

Once in the parking lot I opened the passenger door for her then walked around to the driver's side.

"I guess I'd feel naked without this on," she said indicating her seatbelt as I started to drive away.

"What," I asked absently. My mind was racing along far from the current conversation we were having. "...oh, yeah, the seatbelt. I never wear one."

"Yeah, I noticed that," she said.

'I've been hoping that if I get in an accident," I thought *"I would get slung through the windshield and killed. With any luck all of that is about to change."*

I pulled the truck over to the side of the road not far from work and shut off the engine.

"There's something I want to tell you," I said turning in my seat to face Christy "I love you. I've loved you for a very long time, and I want you to know that, no matter what else happens." She looked at me blankly. I had no idea what was going on in her head, but at this moment it didn't matter. Words were falling out of my mouth like idiots in barrels over Niagara Falls, and I couldn't have stopped if my life depended on it. And I was pretty sure it did.

"I know that I'm not really in a position to lay this on you," I continued totally undaunted "and I have absolutely no intention of getting you wrapped up in some seedy affair with a married man. That's why I'm not going to act on my feelings past this right now. I'm going to fix the situation that I'm in first so things can be right between us from the beginning. I also am not stupid enough to think that I'm the only guy out there that might be chasing you, and I don't expect you to wait around until I get all of my personal bullshit worked out. But I also want you to know that that's ok, because if you can't wait, and you do find someone else before I'm out of my mess, I'll just find you when it's all over and take you away from whoever you're with."

Christy just looked at me expressionless.

"OK," I said "I said it...you know now because I said it. I guess we can go back to work now."

I started the truck and put my seat belt on.

"I love you too," she said.

I smiled as I put the truck into gear.

I still didn't kiss her, in fact to that minute I still hadn't touched her. I knew that the instant I touched her all of my resolve to do the right thing would go flying out the window. I couldn't afford to let that happen. This was the beginning...or the end of my life right here.

Period.

THIRTY:

Mary had held the purse strings for quite a long time, and she made sure that I only had enough cash to put gas in my car for work. She never said that, but it was a simple fact. If I asked her for cash she would want to have an accounting of whatever had happened to what she had given me before. She used the fact that she had a household to run as an excuse but I knew the facts. It was just one more level of control. If I was ever going to escape from this hell I was going to need some initial financing.

I squirrelled away as much as I could. If Mary and I went to the ATM to withdraw cash, I always palmed $20 or so. I knew that the less money I ask for on a more frequent bases the easier it was to hide the excess. Every once in a while I would take the ultimate chance and withdraw a couple hundred dollars out of the bank on my way to work. Mary never checked the bank statement, that was why we were in the horrible financial state we were in, but I couldn't chance her finding a large amount of money missing.

At work Christy and I acted as if the conversation on the way to "breakfast" had never happened. We talked about things just like we had before, I clandestinely listened to Jimmy Buffet until I dreamed about it, and I made my preparations.

One of the things that I wanted to do was make sure that the house was finished before I left for good. I can't explain it, but I didn't want to think that I left Mary with a half-finished house to go along with a broken marriage. So every day I painted, laid tile, cut grass, planted plants, went to work, and hid money. The only thing new was that I was doing all of these things with a purpose now.

Then the only thing that could have happened to derail my plans happened. Christy took two weeks off of work for vacation. I knew that it was coming. In fact the last night that we worked together I walked her out to her car to say goodbye. We were standing next to her car, a warm breeze was wafting through the trees, and the sky was an incredible blanket of stars. She was saying something, but all I was concentrating on was her mouth. Beautiful full lips that needed no lipstick to make them inviting, gently parting as she spoke revealing a hint of perfectly straight white teeth. Then they would close again as she formed another word, softly coming together and parting again. It was all in mind numbing slow motion, and I soaked breathlessly in their river of promise.

That was when I abandon all sense of decorum, planning, and control. I placed my hands against her car on either side of her head and moved my face toward hers. Our lips touched and it felt just as I knew it would. There were no fireworks, or bands playing, or any other hookie Hollywood staged theatrics. There was simply the softness that I knew would be there although I had never felt if before. It wasn't the softness of her lips, or the tenderness of her kissing me back, although all of those things were true. It was a deeper softness of the sole, a softness that welled up through her, and emanated from the pours of the skin on her face, reaching into my heart caressing my weary emotional self. It scared the hell out of me at the same time it was exhilarating. It was exhilarating for all of the obvious reasons, but it was one of the most frightening things I had ever encountered because it planted a feint glimmer of something in my being that I hadn't felt for years. I felt hope.

I moved back to look into her eyes and they were closed. They actually were closed for a while. I know that when they opened I had that dopey crooked smile on my face that used to be perpetually planted there when I was in grade school. I kissed her one more time then stood up straight.

"I'll miss you while you're gone," I said.

"I'm going to miss you too," she said sadly.

I promise that it's not always going to be like this," I told her.

"I know," and with that she got in her car and drove out of sight.

We all planed our vacations months in advance, and the fact that she was going to be gone for two weeks was no surprise to me. I just couldn't deal with the fact that the only thing that had any kind of meaning in my life was taken from me, and kissing her like that wasn't going to help. Going to work now was simply the drudgery of going to work. There was no promise of stimulating conversation with an intelligent person that just so happened to also be beautiful.

There was no smile.

There were no laughing eyes.

There was nothing.

It took everything I had just to drag myself from one day to the next. I was pretty certain that I was about to screw up on a grand scale.

...and I was so right.

After about ten long gut wrenching days of this I was laying tile on the back porch. Every mundane minute that passed by was filled with thoughts of Christy, and how long it was going to be before I was able to see her again. I thought that Mary might be starting to catch on to the fact that something was going on with me, but the fact was that her daily actions were so unstable I never really knew what the hell was going on in her head.

The glass sliding door opened, and Mary was standing there not saying anything. She was just looking at me like she was trying to read my mind. I was sure that she could, and I was screwed.

"I'm going to the store," she said plainly. "Is there anything you want me to bring back for you?"

"Um, no thanks," I said trying to hide my distraction.

"Don't do anything bad while I'm gone," she said lightly.

"I wouldn't think of it," I smiled.

Mary stopped there for a moment with a blank expression on her face studying me like she was trying to unlock something from deep inside my mind. After a few seconds she smiled, closed the door and drove out of the driveway.

I listened until I heard the sound of her engine fade away as she went around the corner. Then I waited for a few minutes to be sure she hadn't forgotten something, or changed her mind and turned around. After I was sure she wasn't coming back I sprang into action. I ran into the garage and ripped a plastic garbage bag from the roll I had sitting on a shelf above the washer and dryer. At first the bag didn't rip free of the others as I tore it from its resting place and the entire roll tumbled to the floor, and unrolled itself down the driveway as I ran into the house. I hurried into the bedroom and started ripping clothes out of the closet indiscriminately jamming them into my black plastic bag.

I ran out of the garage and flung the bag unceremoniously into the back of my truck. Then I ran back into the garage like a fire fighter looking for kids in a burning building. I grabbed a few woodworking tools, and tossed them into the truck. I figured that Mary would really be able to take every single dime that I made just like she said she would, so I was going to need to supplement my income with construction work.

My mind raced. What was I forgetting? I knew that it was now or never and I was only going to be able to get one shot at this. Then it hit me…the money! I ran back into the house and ripped the $5000.00 I had hidden in the closet out of its resting place, and I ran back out to the driveway and jumped in the truck. I knew exactly where I was going, but the direct route to Christy's house would follow the same path that Mary had just driven down. I turned the other way, and took a more circuitous route.

As I was driving I thought that it might be a giant mistake to go directly to Christy's house. I had no idea if I was being followed, and I had to make sure that she was protected first and foremost. I drove instead to a nearby Howard Johnsons, got a room, and called Christy.

"I'm out," I said.

"You're what?" she asked hesitantly.

"I'm out…I left," I said "I'm at the Howard Johnsons."

"I'll be right there," she said "what room are you in."

"222."

The phone went dead.

I don't remember how long I waited, but it seemed like an eternity. I paced back and forth in the room thinking about what my next move would be. I knew beyond a question of a doubt that Mary was going to hunt me down, and work was probably the first place she'd look. But on the other hand I didn't want to find out the hard way that she was out cruising the streets looking for me. I couldn't allow Christy to be placed in danger like that.

I was lost in all of that back and forth when there was a knock at the door. Without thinking I pulled it open. There stood

Christy with the biggest smile on her face that I have ever seen on another human being. We fell into each other's arms and kissed, then we just stood there looking at each other giggling like little kids that just smooched on the playground.

"Let's go get something to eat and we can talk," I said.

"Let's go," she said.

"We'll take your car," I said. I didn't mention that this seemed like a good idea so mine wasn't spotted by a psychotic lunatic.

We went to a trendy restaurant in an even trendier part of town. Conversation and beers flowed nonstop. Anything I told you at this point that we talked about would be purely made up because I vacillated between being hopelessly in love with the woman sitting across from me, and being out of my mind worried about what was going to happen next.

As Christy went home that night I told her that I was going to go talk to a friend of mine, and see about moving in with him, but I would see her in the afternoon. She said that she had to do some work with the youth group at her church but we could get together after she was done with that. We made a date for 6 PM.

As they say, If you want to make God laugh…make plans.

THIRTYONE:

I drove out to my friend's house after talking to him on the phone. I told him what was going on, and to my surprise his only comment was "it's about time." He had a great place but it was on the other side of town. But I guess fugitives can't be choosers. On the bright side, I was pretty sure that Mary would get lost if she ever tried to drive all the way up there and find the place.

After I dropped off what few belongings I had at my new temporary residence I drove off for work. It was my day off, and other than the fact that I had to let them know where they could get hold of me if they needed to I can't really remember why I would go out there if I wasn't working. I just know that I did.

When I got in the building one of the guys that I work with pulled me into one of the union offices.

"I don't know what's going on," he said smiling…he was always smiling, "but your old lady has been calling here all day looking for you."

"And?" I said.

"And my ass," he said back "you've got to do something about that. She's calls about every half hour asking for you, and it's starting to piss off management."

"I'll take care of it," I said.

I called Mary from one of the outside lines at work.

"Hello," she said, sounding waaaaaay too under control.

"It's me," I said.

"No shit."

"I'm not coming back."

"Where are you?" every word was clipped and measured.

"I'm at work. We can work out what's going to happen next, but I'm not coming back."

"Work what out?"

"Money, who gets what, those kinds of things."

"I'm not working shit out with you over the phone."

"I'll come down there, but I'm not coming back. I'm only coming down there to straighten out financial matters."

The phone went dead.

I got in the truck and headed for what used to be home. I didn't know for sure what awaited me there, I only knew that I wasn't going back to her, and if going there to confront her face to face was going to facilitate the separation, so that I could spend the rest of my life with Christy then it was a small price to pay. However, that's easy to say when you haven't seen the price tag yet.

I pulled into the driveway and the house already seemed foreign to me. I had a knot in my stomach that threatened to push everything in it out onto the pavement, but I had the steely eyed determination of a man fighting for his life in armed combat. Little did I know that that analogy was going to be real close to accurate in just a few minutes.

As soon as I walked in the house Mary was standing in the foyer, her face a Technicolor rainbow of wrath and self-pity.

"I'm not coming back," I said, "I've had enough, and I'm not coming back."

"Really," Mary said. She physically looked like she was crouching down getting ready to spring on a wounded animal. Her lower lip quivered and her hands were balled into fists so tight that all color in them was either bright blood red or dead fish white.

"Really, it's over, and there's really nothing to talk about anymore."

"Is that right?"

"Yes it is."

"So is that all you have to say then?"

"Yeah, unless you have something else you want to talk about. If not, I'm going to leave."

"Just like that huh?"

"Yes."

I moved to the door and Mary reached out and grabbed my shirt so quick I never saw her hands move. She pulled me toward her and slammed me back into the wall hard enough to leave an impression in the drywall.

"This isn't going to change..."

POW! She connected with my face and I staggered back into the kitchen.

"How long is this going to take," I thought *"I have to meet Christy at 6."*

I stole a look at the clock on the wall as Mary punched me in the gut. It was already almost five. I don't remember a lot of the rest of what was said or done. There was a lot of screaming back and forth, and at some point I was standing in the doorway that connected the kitchen to the garage. Mary grabbed me by the shirt that was already half way torn off me and jerked me back through the door. My collar bone slammed into the door frame, and white hot pain raced through my body as I heard the bone break. I stumbled across the living room, and ended up in the bedroom. Mary cocked back to let me have it again, and I caught her fist.

"Hit me again you mother fucking bitch!" I screamed into her face. "Do it God damn it…fucking do it, and see what happens!"

The pain in my shoulder was overwhelming. But more important than my physical pain was the knowledge it was already after 6, and I knew that Christy was going to think that I had changed my mind.

"What are you going to do you pussy?" Mary said. But there was something in her voice that I had never heard before. She had no idea what I was going to do next. Hell neither did I.

"You know what?" she said calmly "Do whatever you want. I don't care. But I know where you're staying, and I'm going to make a few phone calls in the morning, and I'll make sure that his boss knows he has a little cocaine, and drinking problem at work"

"Do what you want, he doesn't have a problem with either of those things, and it will be your word against his."

"You know the truth doesn't matter," she scoffed. "All I have to do is put a reasonable doubt in their minds."

"You're just that big of a bitch aren't you?"

Mary grabbed me again and pulled herself to me as she let out a scream in pain. She had breast reduction surgery not long before this, and the stiches were still fresh. Apparently all of the pulling on me had ripped a few of them loose. She went to lie down on the bed, and I paced the floor in the living room. The opening of the stiches had tossed a bucket of cold water on the heat of the fight, but now I had to decide what I was going to do next. I couldn't go back to the place I was staying because Mary was going to try and ruin him. I couldn't just leave her there with her stitches pulled out, not because I cared, but because I didn't know what she would do if I was gone. Everybody in the neighborhood must have heard the screaming match.

It suddenly became clear to me that my preplanning was flawed to say the least. I was going to have to move back in with Mary, and plan better for my next escape attempt. I was going to have to find a place to hide where even if Mary found me she wouldn't be able to hurt anyone else. But more importantly I was going to have to tell Christy what happened, and that ripped my heart out. During the entire fight all I had been thinking about was her. Where was she? Was she waiting for me? How was she going to take it? My shoulder was killing me, but that was nothing compared to the pain I felt in my heart for her.

My head was swimming, and I don't remember what was said between Mary and I in the aftermath of violence. She had calmed down, and I had told her that I would come back. She went with me to my friend's house to get my things. He wasn't home when I arrived so I just gathered up my shit, and went back to my cesspool with Mary.

THIRTYTWO:

The next day I went back to work. I knew that I was going to make everything right eventually, but I also knew that first I had to break Christy's heart. I saw her in the hallway and the look on her face was the most unbearable thing that I have ever had to witness in my life.

"What happened to you?" she asked.

"Let's go outside," I said to her "we need to talk."

(I've had to take o few days off for this one. I felt a change in me sometime during this writing. An interesting sort of uncontrolled personality switch where suddenly I was just writing this story like it had happened to someone else. I don't like that disconnection because that's how evil continues to exist in this world. People have horrible things happen to them, and then instead of working to change something, they push it out and block it from memory.

However, working up to this part I've had to relive a lot of pain that I caused someone else, and there's no disassociating that for me. Of course the nightmares are back, I knew they would be when I got to this part. I just didn't expect them to be so fucking vivid.)

Christy and I walked out to a small eating area just outside of our building, and I sat down on top of a picnic table facing her. All I wanted to do was run away.

"I went back," I said looking her in the eyes. I don't know if I held her direct, penetrating stare like that for her, or if I did it to punish myself for tearing her apart like that.

"OK," she said looking down at the ground.

She was crushed, and I hated the very existence of myself for being the vehicle that had run over her in such an awful way. My shoulder hurt like hell, and I lavished in the pain of it. I felt as though that was poetic justice.

"I'm going to fix this," I said. She looked up at me. "I screwed up, and left before I had everything worked out. I told her where I was staying like an idiot and she threatened to destroy Bill."

"When did you talk to her?" she asked.

"I went to work to pick something up, and Steve told me that she had been calling all day. So I called, and told her that it was over, and the only thing to talk about was how to work out money issues."

"What did she say?"

"She told me that the only way she was going to talk to me was if I went down there and did it face to face,"

"So did you?"

"Yeah, I went there and there was no surprise that it got pretty ugly, pretty fast, but she said that she was going to destroy Bill and I couldn't let that happen."

"How was she going to do that?"

"She was going to contact the facility, and tell them that she knew he had a cocaine and alcohol problem, and that he did it on the job."

"But that's not true."

"Of course it's not true, but you know how these jackasses operate. All they need is a rumor that something bad is happening with someone, and that's the end of a career."

"So what now?" she asked as she gazed off into the distance.

"Nothing changes," I said. She turned around to look at me. "Well, nothing changes from the way it was before all of this. I don't want you to ever have a reason to feel as though I'm using you or leading you on, so no more of what happened the other night until we can be together forever."

She folded her arms and looked at me quizzically. "Really?" she said with her head slight cocked.

"Yeah, really," I said "I've already screwed this up once because of being overly eager, and you need to know in your heart that I'm serious."

"OK," she said.

"There's just one thing," I said.

She gave me a look like *"here it comes"*.

"This time I'm going to ask you to wait for me," I said. "Just give me a few weeks to get things right, and we can start putting all of this behind us."

"I can do that," she said. "I have to get back up to work."

She started to walk back into the building. "I'm so sorry," I said "but I promise I'll spend the rest of my life making it up to you."

"A few weeks," she said pointing at me for emphasis. She still had that sly smile on her face.

"I promise," I said.

She hesitated for a second then turned, and walked inside. I sat there on the picnic table looking off into nothing as my mind raced at light speed trying to figure a fool proof plan that would circumvent Mary's crazy, and keep it from splashing on anyone else, most importantly Christy. I would have to find an iron clad place to go live. Preferably with someone else, so that I would have an alibi when Mary started getting the police involved with false assault reports…or worse. I really had no idea what she might be capable of once I was gone. I would also have to find someone that was untouchable, somebody that had nothing to lose from Mary, and could just brush off her threats. I had to get the house really finished. I had to hide the money I had tucked away, and I had to make sure that once I was out I never, ever, ever spent any time alone with Mary again.

THIRTYTHREE:

Things at work with Christy went back to being pretty much the same as before, with the exception of a hint of underlying tenseness that was certainly understandable. Christy had been through a marriage just like the one that I was trying to remove myself from, and there was absolutely no reason for her to trust me. But she did. I imagine the fact that I never brought up what I was doing to try and extricate myself from my mess didn't help, but the way I looked at it if I was actually doing something then I didn't have to talk about it all the time. In my experience talkers were not doers.

At home things were far from back to normal aside from the constant fighting. Mary had become almost an invalid because of her broken stitches that had to be redone. I know she felt that if she could show herself as being completely dependent on me, then I wouldn't threaten to leave again. I guess that beating the hell out of me to force me to stay went out the window when I threatened to pound her ass in retaliation.

Everyday Mary made sure that I never left her sight. If I was working in the yard I would see her looking out the window at me every once in a while, just making sure that I hadn't run away through a hole in the fence like an insolent pet. If I was a few minutes late coming home from work she would be standing in the front yard when I got home demanding to know where I had been.

So one night during dinner I decided to try and do this the right way one time and see where it got me. If the conversation went the way I thought it would I had plan two waiting in the wings ready to jump into action.

"I think we should talk about what happened the other day," I said.

"Why?" Mary said suspiciously.

"Because there is a lot to that that we can't just leave lying around. It's not healthy," I said.

"When did you start worrying about what was healthy here?" she asked. I knew that I was getting ready to open a door better left closed. But if I did this right I could leave free and clear, and not have to spend all of my time looking over my shoulder.

"We have done nothing but fight for the last 11 years," I said.

"If you had any idea how to take care of a woman it would have never been like that."

"I know, but that's just my point. If I can't even begin to give you the things you need from a man or a husband then why would you want to be forced to stay with someone that made you feel as bad as you do here."

A cloud passed over Mary's face, and I could almost hear her calculating her next move. I had already left, and told her I wasn't coming back. When she got violent I made it clear that the days of pounding my ass were over until she could drive me back into the cave I was living in before.

She started to cry.

I didn't see that coming but it was almost comical. Mary was so transparent that sometimes I had a hard time taking her seriously.

Out of all the things she had at her disposal she was going to use wounded, helpless female to get what she wanted. I wondered if she had ever used that on any of the boyfriends she had over the course of our relationship.

"I just want you to take care of me," she sobbed.

"I try to every day, sweetheart," I said, *sweetheart* sticking in my throat like wet cement. "But I always seem to fail. Why would you want that? If I was gone you could get what you want."

"That's your answer?" she said, wailing as tears streamed freely down her face. "For eleven years you shit all over me, and now your answer is to walk out?"

"Not walk out," I said, *run like and ape with his ass on fire,* I thought "let you have what you want, finally."

She was wailing mostly incoherently now about every wrong that had ever been committed against her by me. Amazingly though she never made a move to get out of her chair. She didn't run into the kitchen to start getting drunk, she didn't run into the bedroom and slam the door, and most amazing she never made a threatening move toward me.

"Look," I said "I just wanted to give you an opportunity to have the life you always wanted, with someone that you could respect, someone that didn't have all the negative baggage that I have."

"I don't want anyone else," she said "I've invested too much time, effort, and energy in you to just drop it now, and act like it never happened. I've always seen a potential in you, and you've always fought me while I tried to make you a better person, and now you're just going to give up and walk out…just like that? We took vows…vows to always stay together. Obviously that didn't mean anything to you, but it sure as hell meant something to me."

"OK, OK, OK," I said "I didn't mean to get you upset. I just wanted to try and make you happy, because you're obviously not happy with me."

"That's your fucking fault!" she screamed "and to fix it you're going to walk out on me? I don't believe you! Do you think that any of the other husbands around here are giving their wives the gift of walking out right now, like you're trying to give me? What the hell is the matter with you anyhow? I just want you to love me enough to change, and be the husband that everybody else is apparently good enough to have. I don't even expect you to be anything special; just care enough to be as good as everybody else. But you can't even do that for me can you…"

I don't know if you can yahda, yahda, yahda, an argument, but if you can this would be the place where you would insert it. The endless stream of hurt feelings, accusations, and demands went on well into the night. It was just like old times, but minus the hitting and violence. I also knew that it would be just a matter of a short time before it started all over again just like it had been before. Mary went to bed at some point, and actually went to sleep. The actual verbal bludgeoning might have been over uncharacteristically quickly, but crazy was still skulking in the shadows.

Then, about three days later I walked in the house after work, and there was Mary sitting in the living room. The late afternoon sunlight spilled into the room casting easy shadows on the white bathrobe she had obviously been sulking in all day, and the soft yellow rays of the setting sun splashed her blue green face in a cavalcade of interesting color that marked my imminent demise.

On the coffee table in front of her was a stack of $20 dollar bills. I'm no money expert but it looked like there might be about $5000.00 sitting there under her watchful glare.

"You want to explain this to me?" she asked.

"I had taken that when I left, and I guess I never put it back," there was no need to try and deny what it was, or make like I had no idea what was going on. I knew she had been rifling through my things trying to find out where I had been when I ran away, and she found the stash that I was keeping for my next breakout.

"What are you going to do with it now?" she asked darkly.

"Well, now that I know it's still in the house I guess we should put it back in the bank," I said as matter-of-factly as I could.

Of course there was a fight. There was, and always would be a fight. But there were two very odd things about this fight. First, I could see that even though Mary wanted to beat the shit out of me with every fiber of her being, she resisted. Second, there was more begging for me to be a real man then there was reliving stories about what a piece of shit I had been. I think that Mary knew she had lost control, and she was trying to figure a way to get it back again. I also think that she knew I was going to bolt again the very first opportunity that I got. I'm sure she had no idea how to handle this since she had never been anything other than in complete control of me right from the beginning.

There was no question that eventually the brutality would start again. I could sense it swimming just below the surface. Even during this conversation I could make out the faint outline of one fin that was just getting ready to come out of the water. But it didn't really matter because my real salvation waited for me at work, and as soon as I figured how to swim to shore faster than Mary could catch me, I was going to be nothing but a distant memory.

Everyday my thoughts were consumed with nothing but Christy, and how I would get out of the mess that I had allowed to swallow me whole. In concert, every day Mary became more suspicious of my activity. One day, I was working in the back yard putting Mexican tile down on one of the patios. I had to move out of the front yard because one of the females on the street was stalking the veldt so I had to hide until she left. It was fairly late in the afternoon, the humidity was 90% and the thermometer hung just above the same number. My dedication to the job was slipping fast, but a usual I would do anything to keep from going back in the house and give Mary an opportunity at target practice.

I had a portable table saw with a masonry blade that I left sitting on the ground so it would be easier to cut tile as I laid it on the concrete slab. I let my thoughts drift off to what I was going to do to get out, and when I was going to do it. I picked up a triangular piece of terracotta and started grinding it into a heart shape with the intension of giving it to Christy the next time I saw her at work. After a few minutes of this I realized that someone was watching me and I looked up at the patio door to see Mary standing there with her arms folded.

She opened the door when I saw her. "What's that," she asked suspiciously.

"Something I was making for you," I answered without even thinking about it.

"What is it" she said.

I handed it to her and she smiled. "Thanks," she said, and went back into the house closing the door.

Later the next day I found where she had put it in her dresser, and I stole it back, took it to work, and gave to the person that it was intended for in the first place. I didn't care at that point. I knew that by the time she discovered it was missing I would be out the door right behind it.

The decision had been made. The plans were in place, and I thought everything was pretty much fool proof. It had to be because this time was my last chance at redemption.

THIRTYFOUR:

I was putting the last coat of paint on the last flower box in the front yard, of the last project that marked an end to the rebuilding of the house after the hurricane. It was the first day of my three day weekend, and I knew without a shadow of a doubt that today it was going to be now or never. Mary came out to the front of the house to make sure that I wasn't doing anything where other women could see me.

"You look like you could use a shopping day," I said.

"Yeah," she said. Clearly she was feeling sorry for herself. It was just as clear as that that night had all of the possibilities of a giant blow out fight. "I'd like to get out for a while."

"Why don't you go to the mall, and look at curtains for the living room," I suggested, "then when you get home we can have a nice dinner together, and decide what we want to do with the rest of the house."

She looked at me like she was trying to figure out what kind of shit I was pulling. That wasn't odd though, Mary had always looked at me like that whenever I suggested she get some time to herself.

"Go ahead," I reassured her, "by the time you get back I'll be done here and we can spend the rest of the evening together."

Mary agreed and slunk back into the house to get ready to go. My mind was speeding down the track like A J Foyt on crack. I just had to keep up the bullshit level until Mary was gone. She was constantly reactive and intuitive, like a predator on the hunt, so one false move or a hint of something out of place and I was screwed. The next few minutes walking through this dance of deception was going to be the most important thing that I had ever done in my life, and I couldn't show my hand.

Eventually Mary came back to the front yard looking like a woman being forced to walk to the electric chair. The façade wasn't for any special reason, it was simply the motif that she had chosen for the day, and we were both going to get to partake when she got home.

"I'm going to go now," she said.

"OK sweetheart," I said cheerily…but not too much so." Drive carefully, and call me if you need anything."

Mary slid into the Corvette, checked her hair in the mirror, adjusted her sunglasses, smiled faintly at me, and backed out of the driveway. I waved as she pulled away from the house, and I went right back to painting. As Mary turned around the corner I made absolutely sure that I wasn't watching her go. That would have brought her right back to the house.

I checked my watch and waited for five minutes to make sure…again…that she wasn't coming back. I went into the house and left Mary a note, I don't remember now what I wrote but it was something like *I'm leaving for good…you deserve better than me…I'm taking $5000 out of the bank, and that will leave $30,000 dollars for you to take care of bills until things are straightened out between us.* I hoped that telling Mary that she should have something better than me, and the fact that I left all of that insurance money for her would keep her from hunting me down.

That's what I hoped for anyway.

I ran through the bedroom collecting my cloths, unceremoniously cramming them into another black plastic garbage bag. I ran outside, tossed the bag in the right seat of my truck and went back into the garage to grab some of my tools again. Into the back of the truck they went. I went back into the house to make sure that I wasn't forgetting anything important, because I only was going to get this one chance. It appeared that I had the things I needed, so I hurried out to the truck. I checked the street one more time, then pulled out of the driveway, and drove in the opposite direction of the route Mary had taken when she left just a few minutes before.

I drove to the bank to withdraw the money I told Mary I was going to take. To use one of my father's favorite phrases, I was nervous as a whore in church while I waited in the bank for my money. I expected that at any time Mary would come barging through the door, or possibly she would be waiting for me in the parking lot. I had no idea what I was going to do if she showed up, but I was sure that I wasn't going to get trapped into going back into that house ever again.

The teller handed me an envelope, I thanked her, and headed for the door. As I came out of the bank I felt like Dustin Hoffman in *Dog Day Afternoon* when he comes out to pay the pizza delivery man. I knew Mary was out there someplace, and I was just waiting for all hell to break loose. As I walked toward my truck I was hyper vigilant for any red Corvette that might come flying around the corner with the intension of crashing into me so the driver and I could spend the rest of eternity together.

Quickly I unlocked the door to my truck and climbed inside. I looked both ways in the parking lot; not a red car of any type in sight. I let out a sigh of relief, and wiped a bead of sweat off my forehead. The finish line was in sight, and all I had to do now was stay alive long enough to cross it.

I drove down the street making sure that I followed all traffic signals and speed limits. The last thing I needed to do was get pulled over by the cops. I'm sure that a red S-10 pickup on the side of the road with a police car, complete with flashing lights to mark it, might not have gone un-noticed if Mary should drive by. I kept checking the rearview mirror, and all side streets. Soon Christy's

Townhouse was insight, and I was just a matter of a few yards from my goal.

I pulled into the parking lot, stopped, and checked the street behind me. There was nothing there, but you could never be too cautious when your very life was at stake. I waited there for a few minutes to make sure that no one pulled in behind me. The horizon seemed to be lunatic free, so I pulled into a parking spot in front of Christy's condo. Still, I wasn't sure that somebody wasn't going to drive up and piss on my parade so I waited in the truck for a little while to give anyone that was following me the chance to reveal themselves. Still there was nothing there.

I got out of the truck and walked up the sidewalk to Christy's condo. Through the half glass door I could see her there watching television. I turned around to look behind me one more time, and the irony of that move wasn't lost on me. Right at that moment behind me was my past, and I was still going to spend a lot of time looking over my shoulder, but in front of me was a new future that was going to be whatever I decided to make out of it. The enormity of that knowledge washed over me, exhilarated, and scared the hell out of me all at once.

I knocked, watched as Christy jumped off the couch, and ran to the door. When she opened it I threw my arms around her vowing to myself that I would never let anything come between us again, no matter what.

For the rest of that day we talked about what was going to happen next, and I could tell by the things that Christy was saying that she didn't have the full picture of just what type of loon she was going to be dealing with. Unfortunately she would find out in short order. The next day Christy went with me as I put the second part of my plan into motion. I realized that I had the perfect roommate for the job. I just had to convince him to let me live there for a little while.

Jim was a co-worker, and a good friend to both of us. He was gregarious, edgy and more than just a little bit "out there". He had some problems in his past that included armed robbery, assault, assault with intent to do bodily harm, and breaking and entering, to name a few of the more important of his job qualifiers, and had spent a little time behind bars where he fixed his drug dependency issues, but held tightly to alcohol.

He was exactly the thing I was looking for in a roommate.

I called Jim and asked if it was OK for us to come over because I had a favor to ask of him, and in true fashion he told me to feel free without even asking what I wanted out of him. When we walked into his house I knew that this was just the place I was looking for. They only furniture in the living room was a bench press with free weights scattered around on the floor, and an impressive set up already slid onto the weight bar resting on the bench bar holders. In the dining room was a table and chairs that looked like they came right out of an episode of "*Leave it to Beaver*", but more importantly on the table was a Smith and Wesson 9mm semi auto that had been torn down for cleaning, and a model 1911 45 that was ready to go. Sitting around these weapons were about thirty bullets of each bore size all standing in a row like lethal little solders standing by to load up and get their marching orders.

We followed Jim into the "TV" room where a television sat purposefully on some type of crate. Jim sat down on the sofa and motioned for us to make ourselves comfortable on the only other furniture in the room…two old nylon web lawn chairs.

"So," Jim said "what can I do for you this fine day?"

I laid everything out for him right down to the fact that there was no way that Christy and I could move in together because I had to protect her from the nut.

After I finished, Jim just sat there smiling at Christy, "I guess this means there's no hope for the two of us then is there?" he finally said.

"No," Christy said, "there isn't."

"Well I guess it's a done deal then," Jim said as he slapped himself on the thighs and stood up. "You can toss your shit in that back bedroom there, and make yourself at home."

I told him that I didn't know how long these things were going to take and that I didn't feel comfortable sponging off him for free, so I made a deal with him to help him rebuild the damaged house he had bought after the hurricane as a repayment.

THIRTYFIVE:

After three days of planning and execution everything was in place. I was living in the man cave with the consummate, "if you can't eat it, or fuck it, then kill it," dude. I hadn't been to, or called work, so there had been no communication with Mary, and I was working pretty hard trying to find a lawyer so I could get things rolling. But on the fourth day I had to go back to work, and that's when things took an ugly turn.

Again...

The facility I worked in was supposed to be secure. Hell, I needed a secret clearance just to be employed there. Consequently, the parking lot was also supposed to be secure, and usually it was. But when I arrived for the afternoon shift that day the first thing I noticed was that the security gate was stuck open. As I pulled in to park the second thing I noticed was Mary's car sitting in the middle of the lot. Thank God Christy and I weren't living together and consequently hadn't driven in together.

I parked, got out of the truck and started walking toward the facility door. Of course I was cut off by the Corvette. Mary's oldest son was driving, and of course Mary was in the right seat. She rolled the window down and looked to all outward appearances like someone that had just been told that there child had been raped, and then torn apart by wolves. She was all laid back in the seat, and blubbering nearly incomprehensibly. The last time I saw that many different colors on one person's face it was hanging on a wall in a Picasso exhibit in an art museum.

I don't remember what she was saying, but it went along the lines of 'please come back I'll do anything you want', in a form of begging that I had never heard come out of Mary's mouth EVER, for any reason. I told her that I wasn't ever coming back and that things were over, and she was going to just have to get used to that idea. Every time I would say something like that, a great wail would issue forth from the right seat of the car followed by a gut wrenching "NOOOOOOOOOOOOOOOOOOOOOOOOO". I had seen these kinds of theatrics out of Mary before when she was jacking her ex-husband around, or some neighbor. But it was like somebody pointing a gun at your face. You might have seen it before but it takes on a whole new meaning when you're staring at the business end. As soon as Mary got her prey where she wanted them all promises were tossed in the crapper, and it was right back to life as usual.

All I kept thinking about was the fact that I had gotten Christy a music box as a gift, and it was sitting behind the seat in my truck. If Mary got in there, and I knew she was going to try to, and found that music box the world was going to turn to instant shit right there. Luckily I had locked the door after I got out. There were only two other things I had to worry about. How was I going to rid myself of this side show and go to work, and what was going to happen if Christy came out and tried to talk sense into Mary.

Those things, and the hope that people I worked with weren't going to get to see this and embarrass the hell out of me were all that consumed my thoughts when Mary got out of her car and walked over to my truck.

"What are you doing now?" I asked her.

"I'm going to sit here in your truck until you get off work," she sobbed.

"No you're not," I said "and it wouldn't do you any good any way. I'm not coming back, and there's nothing to talk about."

"Noooooooooooooooooo," she wailed as she jerked on the unyielding door knob.

For someone that was out of control with grief she seemed to know exactly what she was doing. Her son got out of the car and walked toward me.

"It's locked Mary," I said. She spun around and shot me a looked that would have killed a lesser man instantly. I had only called her by her name once since we had gotten married, and that was during a fight. I got a good hot shot in the mouth for my trouble then, and she almost lost control of the character she was playing when I did it this time.

"Just let me sit in there until you come out," she whined.

"No Mary," I said matter-of-factly, "There's no point, and nothing to talk about now, or when I come out of work, or ever…it's over."

"Noooooooooooooooooo."

"Just let her in the truck man," her son said. He was about 25 then and a pretty big guy. Well over 230 lbs, and he liked to fix most social problems with his hands.

"No," I told him, "this is ridiculous, and she's not getting in my truck."

"Pleeeeeeeeeeeease!" Mary begged as she tugged on the door handle.

"Why don't you just let her in man?" her son said, "then you can go in there and you guys can discuss this after you get off work."

"Look," I said. I was starting to get tired of this. "She's not getting in the God Damned truck, and I'm not going into work while you guys are still here. There's nothing to talk about. It's over, I've had enough, I'm not going back, and she's going to just have to get used to it."

Mary jerked back on the door handle one more time, lost her grip and fell on her ass. I just stood there while she sat on the hot asphalt sobbing.

"Why can't you just open the fucking door!" her son screamed in my face.

"Why can't you both get the idea that this isn't going to go your way, and leave," I said to his back as he walked toward his mother.

I thought he was going to help her up, but instead he walked right past her, continued to the left door of the truck and slammed his fist right through the window. Glass shattered onto the parking lot, all over my seat and all over his mother. She never missed a beat. She jumped up off the ground, unlocked the door and got in.

"I'll be here when you come out," she said.

"I'll call the police if you are," I said unemotionally.

"Why do you have to be such an asshole?" her son said as he pushed me backwards.

"I want you to think of one thing," I said "this is a federal facility, and if you keeping showing your ass here you're going to federal prison."

"Hey, fuck you!" he yelled in my face, but at least he was backing away.

He was hurling some more insults at me, but his mother was well over her hysteria as she rifled through the contents of my glove compartment. I thought there was nothing to worry about there as long as she stayed out from behind the seat.

In the middle of this current round of crazy one of my managers walked out, and asked if everything was alright. Apparently one of the people I worked with had told everybody inside that the ultimate clown death match was going on in the parking lot, and he came out to see what the hell was going on. I told him everything was OK, and that it might be a while before I got into work. In retrospect I should have told him right there to call the police and have these nuts carted away. But I was far from being able to take care of myself yet. All I was doing was holding my own. He went back inside and round two of the nut house slam fest was back on.

The thing that I noticed though, was that every time either one of those two needed to be sane there had no problem making the transformation. If someone drove past, or walked through the parking lot, they would collect themselves. That irritated the hell out of me because it was like holding up a giant sign that read "you're being played, asshole!"

The insanity went on for about another hour with Mary going through all my paper work, and her son running interference for her. Finally I saw her take a piece of paper out, fold it up, and stick it in her pocket. I knew that it had the address on it from the house I was living in now, but I really didn't care. She got out of the truck, and I knew that if they were stupid enough to come calling where I lived they would be introduced to Mr. 9 Milley and his little friend 45 Otto.

For three more hours we stood out there in the blazing sun, her trying to bend my unbendable will, him trying to threaten my into submission, and me fending off insults, and pitiful begging. At one point I looked over to the sidewalk that ran between the parking lot and the building, and I saw eight or ten people I worked with just standing there with their arms folded, watching the show. I was surprised they didn't have drinks and popcorn.

Eventually a car full of technicians came back from doing field work, and pulled up right next to Mary. She was standing at the back of her car going on a long out of control rant about how she didn't know what she had done wrong, but she would do anything it took to make things better. Her son just glared at me. As soon as the techs pulled up she instantly stopped her unbridled pouring out of emotion, waited until they all got out of the car and were in the building before she started again.

I was officially done.

"What the hell was that?" I interrupted her blubbering.

"Whaaaaaat?" she whined.

"Those guys pulled up, and you instantly were in control again."

"I don't know what you're talking about."

"You know…*Mary*…that's funny, because I think you know exactly what I'm talking about."

"BUT I DON'T!" she wailed.

"I'm only going to say this once, then you two are on your own. I want you to leave right now. I'll call you after I get off work if it will make you happy, but nothing's going to change."

"Noooooooooooooo."

I held up my hand. "If you stay here I'm going to call the police. It's up to you"

"Let's just go Ma," her son said.

"You'll call me tonight?" she pleaded.

"Yes," I said

They drove off and I went into work four and a half hours late. Of course I called that night just like I said that I would. At 10:30 when my shift ended I went down to a deserted training room and called Mary. I don't remember what was said, mostly because it was all more of the same bullshit that had been said in the parking lot that day. I do remember her son getting on the phone at some point and telling me that he knew his mother was nuts, but he never really knew how bad she was until now. I recognized it for the ruse that it was. He was trying to get me to promise him that I would work with him to get her fixed. But I knew that all the while he was working to get me back in the house just like before. I had seen him play too many people before not to have the full picture of what he was doing.

That would be the last time I would talk to Mary unless it had to do with a divorce or some sort of legal issue. However, it was far from the last time that I would be touched by her insanity, or threatened by her or one of her children.

A few days after this incident I came back to Jims place after work. He was waiting for me in the driveway, which was odd because he was actually rarely home while I was there.

"We have a problem dude," he said. But he really didn't have to say anything at all. It was written all over his face.

"What kind of problem is that?" I asked, because I really had no idea.

"Your old lady was here today with her kid looking for you," he said.

"I'm really sorry about that," I said "They didn't start any shit did they?"

"Not really," he said, still looking stern. "The kid is a big guy but he's mostly a punk, and I can handle him without any trouble, but your old lady is nuts dude, and she scares the shit out of me."

"Yeah, I know that feeling," I said. I knew what was coming next.

"I'm sorry buddy, but you're going to have to find someplace else to live. If you stay here it's not safe for either one of us."

He was right about that, and I guess I felt some sort of vindication that after all of this time it wasn't just me. Even to this guy, dealing with her was like dealing with Charles Manson. One look into those eyes and you knew that you were in way over your head.

I didn't have any place else to go where I thought the person I was living with would be safe so I was pretty much screwed. I only had one alternative left. Christy's condo still had a lot of work that needed to be done on it, and she was living with her parents until it was completed. I knew I could move in there, and if Mary followed me back there I would be the only one caught up in the shit storm. It wasn't ideal but it was my only option. A friend of mine traded cars with me so I could drive camouflaged, and off I went to another hiding place.

THIRTYSIX:

I guess the majority of everything that happened after that was all comparatively inconsequential. I made several phone calls to find an attorney, some of which turned me down because Mary had already called them, and some because they didn't handle family law. The guy that I finally found put up a giant red flag in our initial conversation that I missed completely. We were getting ready to send a bunch of paper work over to Mary's attorney in order to get things started and Norman, my attorney, said that this was just going to be the first battle in a long war. I should have realized that there was no reason for a war at all. Mary and I had no children, I didn't want the house, furniture, or anything else I had left there, and she didn't want anything that I had taken with me. The only thing to fight over was how much alimony Mary would be paid.

But the paper work storm whipped into a full-fledged hurricane, and we were off to the races. There were depositions, and court dates with a general master. We would sit in this office, and the attorneys would grill each of us with totally irrelevant questions. Mary accused me of wearing her cloths, and acting like a woman.

She even testified that she had photos of me wearing one of her dresses and panty hose. She was instructed to produce them in one hearing, and additionally instructed to turn over half of the $30,000.00 I had left in the bank. That produced very interesting results.

When the court date came, instead of bringing the things she had been instructed to she produced a police report. According to the report, Mary had withdrawn all of the $30,000.00 from the bank in the form of cash, and then she hid it in the house under a wicker basket in the living room. At some point, someone apparently having access to the house, broke in and stole only the $30,000.00 and the damning photos. Norman sat there and didn't say a thing, so I took matters into my own hands.

"Was there anything else taken?" I asked.

"You know there wasn't, because you were the one that took it." She spat.

"So you're saying that on the day I left you I took the time to stop at the bank and withdraw $5000.00, leaving $30,000.00 just sitting there. Then for some unknown reason you cash that account in, and hide the money in your house, and then, even though there is no way that I could have known that you would do anything as crazy as hide $30,000.00 under a wicker basket in the first place, let alone take that much money out in cash, I risk going to jail for breaking and entering, find your hiding place, take the money, and photos of me in women's cloths, and steal away into the night."

"That's exactly what you did!"

I looked at the general master, "let's move along with this," he said unenthusiastically.

That was it. Just drop it, and move on.

For some of the court dates Mary would intercept me on the court house steps, and follow close behind me telling me that she was going to have me killed, and that I had better be watching over my back. Other times she would have her oldest son sit next to me in the waiting area before we went into the court room and tell me degrading personal things about myself that his mother apparently told him to say. I was horrible in bed, my penis was small and smelled bad, I used to ask Mary to sodomize me. All of those things were ignorant, irrelevant, and wrong, but I couldn't decide which was worse; the fact that she said those things to her son, or the fact that he repeated them to me.

This battle went on for a few weeks short of a year for no reason other than the fact that we were making the lawyers house payments, and Mary was too stupid to put a stop to it on her end. On more than one occasion I had told Norman that I didn't want one more piece of paper to leave his office asking for information, or another deposition, or anything else. Simply answer what she asked for and get this thing over with.

Mary and I had been to one mediator session already, and I told them all that I wasn't giving Mary a damned dime that the court didn't instruct me to give her. A few weeks later Norman told me that we were scheduled for another mediator session.

"Why?" I asked.

"The court really likes it when people can work these things out themselves," he told me. "If we go to a final hearing without an agreement the court is going to be pretty hard on you,"

I was already paying her $1800.00 a month, temporary alimony and she was getting everything. How much worse could it get?

The day of the next mediator session I walked into Norman's office.

"What kind of car does Mary drive?" he asked me.

I told him and asked why.

"We saw a car just like hers pull into our drive way, someone got out of the passenger side and dropped a severed mouse head in a baggie on our door step," he said.

"Yeah, that sounds about right," I said "I guess she's hanging around with Santeria now."

As we walked through the parking lot to the mediator's office Norman told me that I could expect to pay some sort of alimony.

"Yeah I expected that," I said. "So why are you telling me that now?"

"Did you expect it to be permanent?" he asked offhandedly.

"No I did not," I told him

"Well you will,"

"How much for Christ sake, you know what I'm already paying her now, and she already wants part of my retirement!"

"I don't know," he said as he held the office door open for me, "but something."

We walked into the mediator's office, and there sat Mary with her youngest son, whom the last time I heard was still in the navy.

"You did expect to see me here did you," he said with a threatening smile.

"I'm never surprised by who your mother gets to hold her hand," I said back. I decided right there that I was going to put a stop to this back and forth bullshit, and get on with my life.

The mediator asked Mary to follow her behind a partition, but I could still hear them talking. The mediator told her that the Mary's doctor was not going to make a statement that Mary could never work again. Apparently Mary had gotten drunk, totaled the Corvette, and ended up with a broken leg that needed to be pinned back together. Mary told the mediator that she knew that but she was going to ask the court for a continuance, and more depositions. We had already flung tens of thousands of dollars at this sinking ship, and we were about to start flinging more money that neither of us had. When they returned to the table the mediator asked if she could talk to just the two of us without the lawyers present. We both agreed, and the paper hangers left. I made a few offers to Mary that she flatly refused. The mediator looked at her like she was an idiot, and took her behind the partition again. When they came back out Mary accepted my offer, the lawyers returned to the room and when Norman heard what we had agreed to he went theatrically nuts, and put on a very cheesy front of disagreement. When we left the room Norman never mentioned the deal, how he felt about it or what he thought I should have done. When we went to the final hearing he put on a forced indignation when the judge read the final agreement, and things were over.

Well, divorce proceeding things anyway. Mary continued to harass, and stalk me long after Christy and I were married. Sometime the hose in my front yard would be chopped to pieces, sometimes parts of my front yard would be salted so nothing would grow there for a very long time. I knew who it was because these were all things Mary had done to the neighbors we lived next to, but I couldn't prove it.

Then she started calling Christy at work threatening to have her beaten up in the parking lot as she left work. Christy's boss told her to stop answering the phone, and any calls that came in for her would be screened. That was when Mary called Christy at work pretending to be a detective. Shortly after that Mary was arrested for criminal stalking.

But things didn't end there. One day a few years later I answered the phone and it was a real detective. She told me that Mary filed a police report saying that she had stopped at a traffic light, and she noticed that I was stopped behind her on my motorcycle. Mary reported that I got off the bike, walked over to the driver's window of the car, pulled her through it, and beat the hell out of her. The detective said that she wanted me to come down to the police station so I could answer a few questions. I told her that we were talking now, and I would be happy to answer anything she wanted me to say right there on the phone. The detective persisted but I held my ground. Something didn't sound right here but I could figure out what it was.

Finally she asked me where I was on the day in question. That was the first time I had heard what day it was supposed to have been, and my alibi was simple. My mother had died of cancer away and the night I was supposed to be beating up Mary I was 1500 miles away in a funeral home attending to her funeral. The detective asked if I could prove it and she wanted the phone number of the funeral home. I produced the proof, and the number asking her to call me back after she talked to them.

When the detective called back to tell me that I was in the clear I asked her why she had been so insistent that I come to the station. "Oh," she said "I was going to arrest you for assault and battery."

"Just like that," I said.

"Yep, just like that. I saw the pictures, and someone beat her up pretty good. We take domestic violence very seriously here."

"Just out of curiosity," I asked "what would you have done if I had made those charges against Mary?"

"Well," she laughed "why would you let a woman beat you up like that."

THIRTYSEVEN:

Seven years after the divorce was final my life was perfect and I couldn't have asked for things to be better. Christy and I were very happily married, and we lived in a beautiful house in a very nice part of town. I hadn't even heard Mary's voice in over five years; since she had been arrested. Christy, and I both knew what the important things in life were, and we never argued...about anything. We loved each other very much, and since we not only worked in the same place, we were on the same crew, so we were literally together 24-7, and we both loved it that way. I had a lot of issues to get over after living in the abuse I had been in, but Christy had also lived in a situation like that so she was overly understanding and helpful.

Then one day the phone rang, and it was Mary. She was pissed off because one of the alimony checks I had sent her hadn't been signed, and the bank returned it. She started telling me what a low life lump of shit I was, and how I had destroyed her life. Instantly, in my mind I was right back where I had been when I was married to her. But the worst feeling I had was that I had no right to be where I was, or to be happy at all. I had an overwhelming urge to go right back to living with Mary because that was the only thing that a worthless piece of shit like me deserved.

I got off the phone, and went to Christy telling her everything that had happened, but more importantly every way that it made me feel. Christy could have gotten indignant about my feeling that I should be back with Mary. But instead she understood, because she had endured a phone call similar to that at one time and she felt the need to go right back to her abuser just like I felt. Christy and I talked for hours about how I felt, and she was the only thing that got me through that. There is no question in my mind that if it hadn't been for her understanding and guidance I would have gone right back into the hell that I had escaped seven years before.

I had night mares about being stuck back in that place from the day I left until just last night, 20 years later, and I've come to the realization that I probably will always have one foot permanently stuck in the quagmire of hurt, and hatred that Mary manufactured. The real painful part is the knowledge that there are thousands of women AND MEN out there right now that feel the exact same way that I feel, but more over there are just as many that got that phone call, or chance meeting on the street, or not so chance meeting in a public place, and without the aid and understanding of someone that has lived that life they have gone right back into the abusive situation that they had escaped from.

Harder yet is the knowledge that many of those men and women have escaped one last time as they succumb to a lethal combination of self-loathing, hopelessness, and the availability of a firearm, razorblade, rope, or pills.

There is no question that a man, in a strictly physical sense, is capable of inflicting more damage to a woman that the other way around. Saying other than that would be foolish. But because of this fact, combined with a society that raises men to be less emotional than women and endure negativity, men are less able to "come out of the closet" with their abuse than women are. Granted, both men and women in our society are viewed as weak if they allow someone to treat them this way. The simple truth is exactly what Kris Kristofferson sang in his song "Jesus was a Capricorn", "*Everybody's got to have somebody to look down on, prove they can be better than at any time they choose.*" My mother always said that if a man ever hit her she would be gone in a heartbeat. Then after 30 years of marriage my father punched her, and the first thing she did was justify it as not really being abuse. After all, he might have been an all-out asshole…but he had never hit her before that.

But even as society is judging abused women as week at best, or "asking for it" at worst, at least they are seen as victims. A man that is being abused is looked at as a pussy that somehow had asked for it. After Christy and I were together she talked me into reconnecting with my family because it was "the right thing to do". The day I flew up to see my parents I was devastated to learn that during my absence my mother had contracted breast cancer, and she would be dead within two years. I was sitting in my parent's sun room telling them some of the things that had happened over the course of 11 years. I looked at my mother sitting in her wheel chair, withering away as cancer took her life, and I told them about some of the abuse as a way to get them to understand why I chose to stay away. When I told my father about the first beating I took he laughed, and said "Well, I won't ask you what you did to deserve that." In his mind the only reason that something like that would have happened was because I had cheated on her, or something else, and clearly I must have asked for it.

After I shared a few of the horrors that I had endured I instantly realized that my own parents saw may marriage to Mary as completely normal, and obviously I had done something to fuck up, and cause Mary to beat me. Additionally, the fact that I chose to stay with her after the abuse started showed them that I was weak and gutless. If my own family saw me this way how could I ever hope to get the rest of society to see me as anything different?

That was when I decided to never say anything at all to anyone about my abuse. Unfortunately, I would see a TV "talk show" where a woman was just beating the living hell out of a guy right on stage as he begged her to forgive him some wrong he had done. The entire time this guy was getting hit in the face the audience would be laughing their asses off. Or I would watch the news and see that the president had just signed a legislation dealing with violence against women. Or I hear some personality make a joke about someone being beaten by a girl, and I would be pissed off for days.

I started writing letters to TV shows and newspapers. I wrote op-ed pieces that naturally were never published. Every time I would hear someone make the comment "You should never hit a woman," I would ask for a list of just who the hell it was OK for you to beat on? I was becoming socially unacceptable, but I didn't care. The more I tried to explain to people that domestic violence was not gender bias, the more I got the deer in the headlights look, and the more it would piss me off.

Finally, one day I was talking to my father and we got into the conversation about the boy that had been abducted, and abused. My father's typical response about the kid liking what he got or he would have left angered me mostly because of my father's ignorance, but also because of the fact that this boy could expect to go through life now being judged for something that he had absolutely no control over.

Then, in order to drive his point home, my father said "Well, I'll tell you one thing. I would have NEVER put up with the bullshit out of some bitch the way that you did." I wanted to reach through the phone and strangle the living hell out of him. But then I remembered something that I had mentioned to my wife after she and I had gone out to dinner with him and one of his girlfriends.

"You already do put up with that every day," I told him.

"That's bullshit!" he yelled into the phone "I defy you to tell me one time that I ever let a woman shit on me in any way at all."

So I told him that every time we went out to dinner with him and his girlfriend, in his own words, he was very careful about the way he handled the waitress because he knew that his date would get pissed off at him at make his life miserable when they got back to his house.

"That's not even close to the same thing as her beating the shit out of me like you let happen to you." He said

...like you let happen to you... I let that echo in my head a little. I knew what his opinion was. I also knew that in reality his bravado stemmed from a tiny little voice in his subconscious that said I was right. But he needed to hold on to the fact that he was somehow exempt from screwing his life up like I had. And to that end he was more than willing to fling his own son under the bus.

I felt the same thing after I was held up at gun point while I was pumping gas into my car early one morning. After that incident I realized just how vulnerable I was in general. I was pumping gas, this kid came up and asked me for change for a twenty, and his partner shoved a gun in my side. There was nothing I could have done different to change that. The interesting thing was the fact that when I related my story to other people I was inundated with suggestions to insure that I would never be taken advantage of like that again. Not one person ever said to me "Gee, there was nothing you could have done. I hope that I'm never in a situation like that.

After that conversation with my father I decided that I needed to at least try and do something to change the way polite society viewed male victims of domestic violence. I decided that the only way to do that was put my own story out there and subject myself to public scrutiny. Possibly, if I tell my story, other men in the same situation will be willing to come forward and tell stories of their own. Maybe even some well-known men, and then people will start to realize that the one thing domestic violence is not, is gender bias.

As I've said throughout this writing, this has been one of the hardest things that I have ever done in my life. But, if one man in one bad, or even desperate situation sees what I've written here, and has the courage to either get out, or if they already are out they realize that what happened to them isn't their fault then what I've done here is worth whatever I've had to endure.

(Today as I was working one of my horses in the round pen I received a text message from an old friend. He and I hadn't seen or heard from each other in well over a decade and had happened to connect through a mutual friend on Facebook. When Steve and I worked together he was going through the exact same thing as I was, possibly even worse. During our reconnecting phone call a few days ago we both had brushed over our abused past. Both of us laughed about having a gun pointed at us and begging the attacker to just please pull the fucking trigger. We laughed about being beaten, and his spending the night in jail for taking an emotional, ill-advised swing at his attacker after she had beaten him.

I related this story to my wife afterward, and mentioned that we were each telling stories about the past and laughing our asses off. I told her I knew if anyone else had ever laughed at what I had said I would have been destroyed. I understand this was two men that had no other way of coping with what they had been through, and all of that pain had been bottled up and stomped down for years.

This is the text that I received about an hour ago;

How long the torturous madness has to go on to where there's a gun cocked to ur (sic) forehead. Somehow the second time I wasn't afraid but somehow at peace with it at the time. (not now). I longed for her to pull the trigger. I think that's why she didn't do it. Didn't want to give me something I wanted. I've never told anyone about that shit. My personal secrets. It took a major part of who I was away.

My answer

If you want, I would like to send you a copy of what I wrote. I think maybe it would be good for you. By the way, you're right. The gun was to control you. The fact that you wanted it so bad is why she wouldn't let you have it.

Him.

Maybe our higher power, the aliens, put u here so I can crawl from the wreckage and breathe again. I told my wife last nite how sorry I was for what she went through to bring me to this point. I was fricken ecstatic when you met Christy. I picked up there where you left off.

Enough of my sobby shit, how 'bout them Bears!